HOW CAN GUN VIOLENCE BE REDUCED?

Other books in the At Issue series:

HOW CAN GUN VIOLENCE BE REDUCED?

Laura K. Egendorf, *Book Editor*

Daniel Leone, *President*
Bonnie Szumski, *Publisher*
Scott Barbour, *Managing Editor*

An Opposing Viewpoints® Series

Greenhaven Press, Inc.
San Diego, California

No part of this book may be reproduced or used in any form or by any means, electrical, mechanical, or otherwise, including, but not limited to, photocopy, recording, or any information storage and retrieval system, without prior written permission from the publisher.

Library of Congress Cataloging-in-Publication Data

How can gun violence be reduced? / Laura K. Egendorf, book editor.
    p. cm. — (At issue)
    Includes bibliographical references and index.
    ISBN 0-7377-0800-X (pbk. : alk. paper) —
ISBN 0-7377-0801-8 (lib. bdg. : alk. paper)
    1. Gun control—United States. 2. Firearms—Law and legislation—United States. 3. Violence—United States—Prevention. 4. Violent crimes—United States—Prevention.
I. Egendorf, Laura K., 1973– . II. At issue (San Diego, Calif.)

HV7436 .H69   2002
363.3'3'0973—dc21   2001040932

Contents

Introduction

Compared to other industrialized nations, the United States has a higher per capita rate of fatalities due to firearm violence. In 2000, firearms killed 8,493 Americans, out of a population of over 270 million. By comparison, Great Britain, which has a population of 59.5 million, has averaged fifty-two firearms-related homicides per year since 1997. Australia—a nation of 19 million—reported sixty-five firearms-related homicides in 1999. Japan, with a population of 126 million, had twenty-two firearms-related murders in 1997. Even when these numbers are adjusted for differences in population sizes, it is obvious that the rates of gun violence in America dramatically exceed those in other developed nations.

Gun control supporters maintain that the United States has significantly higher rates of gun violence because its gun control measures are not as strong as those found in Australia, Great Britain, and Japan. The United States has implemented some gun control laws, most notably the Brady Bill, which was enacted in 1994. The bill, named after former White House press secretary James Brady, who was seriously wounded in the 1981 assassination attempt on President Ronald Reagan, instituted a background check and waiting period (replaced in 1998 by a computerized verification system) before a gun can be purchased. Gun control supporters advocate even stricter measures. However, opponents of gun control maintain that the laws in the three nations cited by gun law advocates have not made those countries safer and have instead led to a new set of problems. An examination of the gun laws in different nations can provide a greater understanding of the issue of gun violence and what steps, if any, should be taken to ameliorate the problem.

Australia, Britain, and Japan

Australia strengthened its gun control laws following a massacre on April 28, 1996. Martin Bryant, a twenty-nine-year-old man with a history of mental problems, walked through the resort town of Port Arthur with a variety of assault weapons, shooting fifty-four people, thirty-five of whom died. The Australian government responded quickly. Within two weeks, it introduced legislation that included a registration system for all firearms, a twenty-eight day waiting period prior to purchase, and a ban on the possession, sale, and manufacture of automatic and semiautomatic weapons. A gun buyback program was also enacted in 1996. Under that program, owners of newly banned guns could surrender those weapons to a government collection center in exchange for a check. By the time the program ended in September 1997, more than 650,000 firearms were exchanged for rebate checks totaling more than $267 million.

Gun control proponents claim the buyback program has been a success. According to the Australian Bureau of Statistics, in 1997 there were

2,185 robberies—24.1 percent of all armed robberies—that involved fire-arms. In 1998, that number fell to 1,910 (17.6 percent). The number of murders committed with firearms also fell, from 99 in 1996 (the year of the Port Arthur massacre) to 54 in 1998. In a letter she wrote to the *Washington Post*, Sandi Logan, the counselor of public affairs for the Australian embassy, asserts: "Where firearms are present in violent crimes, the statistics show a drop between 1996 and 1997 from 25.3 percent to 24.2 percent for armed robbery; . . . [and] from 5.3 percent to 2.6 percent for manslaughter."

However, gun rights advocates assert that the Australian policy has not decreased the crime rate. The gun advocacy group Sporting Shooters' Association of Australia (SSAA) contends that the buyback failed because millions of banned weapons remained on the streets. SSAA notes that the people who exchange their guns are most likely not those who would commit crimes. In a December 1997 report on the buyback program, the organization writes: "Is there any evidence that a real criminal who has an illegal firearm for criminal purposes actually surrendered the firearm during the 'buyback'? The thought is naive and preposterous." Indeed, Australian police estimate that only 15 to 20 percent of the nation's illegal firearms were turned in during the buyback program. The SSAA further maintains that, while homicide by firearms has been declining, homicide as a whole in Australia has increased. The National Rifle Association (NRA), an American gun rights organization, has also stated its opposition to the Australian buyback programs. A March 2000 report on its website states that, while murder rates declined, assaults and armed robberies increased throughout Australia from 1997 to 1998.

Australia is not the only nation to respond to a tragedy with stricter gun laws. A massacre in Great Britain led to a change in gun control policy in that country. The nation was shocked when forty-three-year-old camera vendor and freelance photographer Thomas Hamilton walked into a school gymnasium in March 1996, in Dunblane, Scotland, shot sixteen kindergartners and a teacher dead, left another twelve children wounded, and then committed suicide. In response, the Parliament approved the Firearms Amendment Act. The law bans the possession of any handgun that can fire more than one shot at a time or is at least .22 caliber (caliber being the diameter of a bullet); approximately four-fifths of Britain's 200,000 legally registered handguns became illegal as a result. Citizens who returned the newly banned guns received at least $220 per weapon.

An article from the August 12, 2000, *Economist* states that firearm-related crimes fell in Britain from 5,209 in 1996 to 3,143 in 1999. Firearm homicides in England and Wales declined from an annual average of 62 from 1994 to 1996 to 52 per year since then. However, as with the Australian buyback program, the NRA has asserted that Britain's gun control law fails to reduce crime. In a report on the effects of these laws, the NRA states: "Britain's years of lowest gun crime came in an era when gun controls were virtually non-existent. Increasingly stringent gun controls have been followed by increasing gun crime." The International Crime Victims Survey revealed that England and Wales ranked second overall in levels of crime among industrialized nations in 1999.

Japan has an especially low level of violent crime. In 1996, fifteen people were killed by handguns in Japan. Gun control in Japan has a long history; as far back as 1588, peasants were forbidden from owning firearms. At present, only soldiers and police may carry handguns legally. Hunting rifles can be purchased only after a waiting period and background check. Despite these restrictions, the number of serious crimes committed with handguns increased 30 percent in the 1990s, reaching 170 in 1999. In addition, the restrictions have not prevented Japanese from procuring firearms; the police seize more than 1,000 illegal handguns each year. The gun laws have also failed to keep firearms out of the hands of members of the Japanese underworld.

Building on the Brady Bill

Despite the misgivings many Americans have toward applying the gun control laws of other nations to the United States, gun control advocates maintain that building upon the success of the Brady Bill would help further reduce gun violence. According to the organization Handgun Control, robberies committed with a firearm fell by 33.7 percent between 1994 (the year the Brady Bill took effect) and 1998, from 257,483 to 170,611. The rate of gun-related homicides also declined sharply, from 15,463 to 10,977, a drop of 29 percent.

Opponents of further restrictions on gun ownership question the success of the Brady Bill. Thirty-two states were subject to the law, while eighteen states and the District of Columbia were exempt because they had already instituted waiting periods. According to the NRA, the exempt states were more successful at reducing crime. The organization reports that the murder rate declined by 9 percent in Brady states compared to a 16.4 percent decrease in exempt states.

One addition to gun control laws that has been used throughout the nation is buyback programs similar to those instituted in Australia and Great Britain. In 1999, President Bill Clinton proposed a $15 million program aimed at reducing the number of guns in and around housing projects. People bringing guns to local police stations received fifty dollars per weapon; the guns were then destroyed. Between 1999 and 2000, a reported twenty thousand guns were removed from the streets. President George W. Bush's administration ended the initiative in July 2001.

Studies suggest that these programs have had mixed success at keeping the more dangerous weapons away from criminals. For example, an examination of a buyback program in Milwaukee concluded that homicides are most commonly committed with fairly new and large caliber weapons, while the guns returned in buybacks were largely older and of smaller caliber. However, a decline in gun violence in Pittsburgh has been linked to that city's gun collection program. In 1994, the year the program was launched, there were 155 fatal firearm injuries; two years later, the number had declined to 100.

Gun violence is a concern for numerous Americans. As the above arguments suggest, finding ways to reduce that violence is one of the most polarized issues in this country. In *At Issue: How Can Gun Violence Be Reduced?*, the contributors consider the effectiveness of gun control and other methods in stemming firearms violence.

1

Gun Control Will Reduce Gun Violence

C. Emory Burton

C. Emory Burton is a sociologist and retired Methodist minister.

Gun violence is widespread in America; each year thirty-five thousand people are killed, and another two hundred thousand are injured by firearms. In fact, handguns are used in more than 75 percent of all acts of armed violence in the United States. Implementing federal gun control legislation will reduce the availability of handguns, thus reducing gun-related violence. Policies that have helped reduce the spread of handguns include the Brady Bill and lawsuits against the gun industry. Establishing a system of restrictive licensing—including registration and background checks—would also help ameliorate the dangers posed by the ready accessibility of handguns.

On September 15, 1999, a gunman, with no previous criminal record, opened fire with a handgun during a prayer service at the Wedgewood Baptist Church in Fort Worth, Texas, killing seven people, injuring seven others—some critically—and finally taking his own life.

This is only one of several recent incidents involving violence with guns: Columbine High School in Littleton, Colorado; a Jewish community center in Los Angeles; day trading offices in Atlanta; a high school in Georgia. As tragic as these stories are, the sad truth is that firearms kill some 35,000 people every year in the United States, in addition to some 200,000 injuries, many of them serious or disabling.

The extent of gun violence

In 1995, 181 children under the age of 15 were shot and killed in gun-related accidents, according to the National Center for Health Statistics. Hospital emergency rooms treat almost 100,000 Americans each year for gun-related injuries. According to an article in *The Journal of the American Medical Association*, gunshot wounds cost the nation $2.3 billion a year in medical treatment, and almost half of that is paid for with taxpayer's dollars.[1]

｜ Violence in America, first and foremost, is by gun.｜Two out of every three homicides, about half of all suicides, over one-third of all robberies, and one out of five aggravated assaults are committed with a gun, usually a handgun.[2]

There are some 25 million handguns in this country.｜More people are killed and maimed with guns in the United States than in any other major country of the world.｜In fact, the US may well have more gun deaths each year than all other industrialized countries combined.

The figures cited comprise convincing evidence that the proliferation of handguns and their misuse are serious national problems. In spite of the bumper sticker's claim ["Guns don't kill people, people do"], guns *do* kill people, and they do it at an increasing rate throughout the country. A clear relationship between firearms and violent death and crime has been found.[3]

The United States has come to rely on the gun because of history and habit. Our culture encourages a casual attitude toward firearms, and we have a heritage of the armed, self-reliant citizen. The hero of American movies and TV is the man with a gun. Accustomed to firearms, entertained by drama that portray the gun as a glamorous instrument of personal justice, many Americans underestimate the consequences of widespread firearms availability.

In the days of the frontier, many believed the gun was indispensable simply for survival. We no longer live in such times.[4] Today's increased urbanization and interdependence of American society call for a new approach to firearms. If we do not control guns we will continue to suffer the violence they generate, the crime they cause and the injury they inflict.

Most authorities agree that the handgun is the weapon of concern. The revolver and the pistol are the weapons predominantly used in violent crimes. Although only about one-third of the firearms in the nation are handguns, they account for over 75 percent of all armed violence in the United States. Because the handgun is *concealable* it is the major weapon of crime; because it is *available*, it is the instrument used in suicides and crimes of passion.[5]

The majority of authorities claim that the increase in the number of homicides results in part from the increased use of firearms. The accessibility of guns (domestic manufacture of handguns has risen in the last several years) contributes significantly to the number of unpremeditated homicides and to the seriousness of many assaults.

When the number of handguns increases, gun violence increases; where there are fewer guns, there is less gun violence. *A policy that reduces the availability of handguns will reduce the amount of firearms violence.* When attention is focused not on the number of crimes committed but on the proportion of crimes involving guns, an inference can be drawn that control systems that substantially reduce the number of guns are effective in reducing the level of gun violence.

The need for gun control

But the root causes of US violence go much deeper than gun ownership and the question remains: Will strict gun control significantly reduce killings and injuries caused by guns? The evidence seems overwhelming that it would. Curbing the available instruments will reduce the fatalities caused by criminals, even if the motivational and the structural predispositions to engage in crime would remain untouched.

A number of studies confirm that the proportion of gun use in violence rises and falls with gun ownership. An important point is that in areas where gun ownership is high, both the percent of murders committed by guns, and the general murder rate, are high. In general, states with a high ownership of guns have a higher percentage of homicides using firearms.[6]

A policy that reduces the availability of handguns will reduce the amount of firearms violence.

The simple fact is that murder and other crimes committed with firearms occur more frequently where guns are most plentiful and gun control laws least stringent. This applies both to the overall murder rate and to the percentage of murders involving firearms.

A more telling point is that, with two or three exceptions, states do not presently have effective gun legislation. Many of the laws are obsolete, unenforced, or unenforceable.[7] Guns are readily in the grasp of psychotics, incompetents, alcoholics, criminals—nearly anyone who wants them. Major problems result when guns are brought in to a state from the outside and circumvent that state's relatively strict laws. This frustrates efforts at state and local regulation. A good case can be made for replacing our haphazard, poorly enforced, ineffectual state and local laws with stringent and comprehensive federal legislation. The enactment of strong federal limitations is a prerequisite to success of local measures.

The United States is the only nation in the industrialized world that permits the almost unlimited private ownership of guns. Not unexpectedly, the accidental death rates in most other countries are much below those in the United States. Firearms death per 100,000 people (1992-94 data) show: The United States, 15.22; Finland, 6.86; France, 6.35; Australia, 2.94; England and Wales, .46; and Japan, .07. More people are killed in gun homicides in one day in the United States than in an entire year in Japan.[8]

One argument in defense of handguns is that they are needed by the average citizen for protection, especially against burglars. However, a gun is rarely an effective means of protecting the home.[9] The gun-toting homeowner is more likely to get shot than the intruder. It has been estimated that for every burglar stopped by a gun, four to six homeowners or family members are killed accidentally by a gun. About .2 percent of home burglaries result in the firearms death or injury of the intruder by the householder. Furthermore, keeping a gun at home only offers thieves one more item to steal. At least 150,000 guns are stolen every year, most of them handguns.

A popular defense in the argument against gun control is that the Second Amendment guarantees the individual's rights to "keep and bear arms." The initial intent of the Second Amendment was to forbid Congress from prohibiting the maintenance of a state militia. The Supreme Court has ruled five times that the Second Amendment is limited to service by citizens in state militias.[10]

Support for gun control

One of the ironies of American politics is that there is no meaningful national gun control legislation despite the support by sizable majorities for stricter gun controls. A Harris Poll found that 69 percent of the public, and 57 percent of gun owners, want stricter gun control laws. In a CBS News poll, two-thirds of the public said Congress should pass stricter gun control laws this year, and the same percentage would favor registering all firearms. Eighty percent of gun owners favor a three-day waiting period.[11]

The National Rifle Association has successfully opposed most legislative controls over firearms. However the gun lobby is not the omnipotent, monolithic force it is sometimes thought to be. Its membership, 3.5 million a few years ago, is now down to less than three million. There is evidence of a growing number of handgun control organizations at the state and local levels that could eventually lead to meaningful legislation.

Organizations such as Handgun Control Inc. are working to influence the national scene. The Brady Bill has prevented as many as 250,000 handgun purchases since its passage in 1993. By targeting both the supply and demand for guns, the city of Boston went more than two years without a single young person dying from gunshot wounds. Enforcing a law against possessing both guns and drugs, the city of Richmond seized 512 guns and sent 215 violators to jail; homicide and robbery rates went down 30 percent. It is now illegal to sell guns and ammunition in Los Angeles County. Lawsuits against the gun industry claim they lack safety devices in their products, and make it too easy for criminals and juveniles to obtain guns. Most mainline professional police associations, and almost all major medical associations, now favor more effective gun control.[12]

> *More people are killed in gun homicides in one day in the United States than in an entire year in Japan.*

At the very least, ownership and possession of all handguns should be restricted to those who meet certain eligibility requirements, who can establish a clear need for the weapon, and can demonstrate their competence in using guns. Ownership of every gun would be registered, just as ownership of every automobile is now registered. The background of each applicant would be investigated, a photograph and fingerprints taken, and a test administered to determine the applicant's knowledge of handgun use and storage safety. Such a standard of restrictive licensing, as recommended by presidential commissions on violence, would reduce substantially the handguns now in civilian hands.

Of course effective handgun legislation would take some effort, as would any constructive social proposal, but it would be less costly than some have indicated. The focus is on handguns, which comprise only 35 percent of all guns. The cost per application under restrictive licensing may be offset by the smaller number of applications generated. While an excellent case can be made for banning handguns altogether (with some exceptions like the police and security guards), it would not mean that existing handguns would be confiscated. And it would not affect rifles or shotguns.

The United States pays a terrible price for its heritage of guns. They have scarred our national character, marking many of the most terrible moments in our history. Guns bloody the present and imperil the future. The time has come to come to grips with this national menace once and for all. To allow gun ownership to increase unchecked would mean a continued and greater loss of lives.

No other form of personal violence reflects the national negligence that has allowed the misuse of this powerful weapon to escalate so far. The price for not taking strong effective action is more than our cities and our society should have to bear, and it would not be honoring the Christ who came that we might have life and have it more abundantly.

Notes

1. Quoted in column by Derrick Jackson, August 17, 1999; also see Newton, David E., *Gun Control: An Issue for the Nineties* (Enslow Publishers, Hillside, N.J., 1992), p. 103.

2. Newton (1992), p. 39.

3. Carter, Greg Lee, *The Gun Control Movement* (Twayne Publishers, New York, 1997), p. 3; Cook, Philip J., "The Effect of Gun Availability on Violent Crime Patterns," pp. 130–147 in Nisbet (1990), p. 131; Wintemate, Garen J. Stephen P. Teret, and Jess F. Kraus, "The Epidemiology of Firearms Deaths Among Residents of California," pp. 245–250 in Nisbet (1990), p. 249; Newton, David E. (1992), p. 37.

4. Newton (1992), pp. 19–22.

5. Hofstadler, Richard, "America as a Gun Culture," pp. 25–34 in Less Nisbet (ed.), *The Gun Control Debate* (Prometheus Books, Buffalo, 1990), p. 60.

6. Hofstadter (1990), p. 27.

7. Hofstadter (1990), p. 33; Zimring, Franklin E., "Handguns in the 21st Century," pp. 177–186 in Nisbet (1990), p. 180.

8. Wouters, Jorgen. ABC News, June 19, 1998; Newton (1992), pp. 72–73.

9. The best source here is Yeager, Matthew G., "How Well Does the Handgun Protect You and Your Family?" pp. 213–238 in Nisbet (1990); also Hofstadter (1990), p. 59.

10. Wouters (1998); Carter (1997), p. 24.

11. Connelly (1999); Newton (1992), p. 75.

12. "Guns in America: An Editorial," *Newsweek*, August 23, 1999; Carter (1997), pp. 103–104.

2

Gun Control Will Not Reduce Gun Violence

Phyllis Schlafly

Phyllis Schlafly is a columnist, lawyer, and president of the Eagle Forum, a conservative organization that supports individual liberty, family integrity, and private enterprise.

Despite the claims made by its advocates, gun control will not reduce firearms violence. Supporters of gun control propagate lies, including inaccurate statistics on the number of children killed each day by guns and the assertion that access to guns at home leads to an increase in violence. These lies disguise the fact that laws imposing waiting periods and background checks do not reduce crime. However, registration can lead to gun confiscation and the possible loss of freedoms, as shown in the history of China, Cuba, and Germany. Gun control in Britain and Australia has resulted in an increase in armed crime. The United States should not follow the lead of those nations and instead should recognize the importance of the Second Amendment and the long-standing American belief that gun ownership preserves liberty. The only way to reduce gun violence is to pass laws that give citizens the right to carry firearms. Criminals are less likely to commit violent acts if they believe their victims could be armed.

The Million Moms March was not a grassroots uprising of mothers but a slick media event orchestrated by Bill Clinton's public relations experts and led by Donna Dees-Thomases, who worked for Democrats in Congress, contributed to Hillary Clinton's campaign and is the sister-in-law of Susan Thomases, a top Clinton adviser. The contrived nature of the campaign was evident in the cozy meeting with the President, extravagant television coverage, multi-page color "ads" disguised as "news" in national magazines, and the distribution of color brochures in airports.

The anti-gun moms pretended to model themselves on Mothers Against Drunk Driving, but those mothers are smart enough to go after criminally reckless drivers, not against automobiles. The anti-gun moms

From "The Media Campaign Against Gun Ownership," by Phyllis Schlafly, *Phyllis Schlafly Report*, June 2000. Copyright © 2000 by Phyllis Schlafly. Reprinted with permission.

either aren't smart enough to see that kids are killed by criminals not by guns, or they are just trying to elect Al Gore. The march was such phony political theater. The Associated Press reported that Bill Clinton had "tears in his eyes" when he talked to the Marching Moms (who, of course, didn't number anywhere near a million).

Gun control lies

The march was advertised as growing out of mothers' outrage at the large number of children who are killed by guns. But Professor John Lott Jr., senior research scholar at the Yale University Law School and author of *More Guns, Less Crime*, has exposed the blatant lies in the statistics bandied about by the President and the press, such as the oft-repeated lie that 12 children a day die from guns. Most of the "children" in the statistics on kids killed by gunfire are 17-, 18- and 19-year-olds killed in gang or drug wars in high-crime urban areas. It is unrealistic to think that trigger locks or waiting periods would have any effect in stopping those homicides.

The Centers for Disease Control could identify only 21 children under age 15 dying from accidental handgun deaths in 1996. But 40 children under the age of five drown in water buckets every year and another 80 drown in bathtubs. Are we going to demand that water buckets and bathtubs be locked up and fitted with safety catches? Many more children are killed or injured every year from cars, drowning, fires, and even toys than from guns. The risk of a child drowning in a swimming pool is 100 times greater than the risk of dying from a firearm-related accident.

The Columbine killers violated at least 17 state and federal gun-control laws among the 20,000 gun-control laws on the books today. Does anyone think that Eric Harris and Dylan Klebold would not have known how to unlock their guns, or that a waiting period would have made a difference in the murders they planned months in advance? None of the proposals for trigger locks, waiting periods or gun-show restrictions would have stopped Harris and Klebold.

The only policy that effectively reduces public shootings is right-to-carry laws. Allowing citizens to carry concealed handguns reduces violent crime. In the 31 states that have passed right-to-carry laws since the mid-1980s, the number of multiple-victim public shootings and other violent crimes has dropped dramatically. Murders fell by 7.65%, rapes by 5.2%, aggravated assaults by 7%, and robberies by 3%. On the average, murder rates in states without concealed-carry laws are 127% higher than in states having the broadest carry laws.

The United States has a population of 270,000,000, and 600,000 to 750,000 people are in law enforcement. It is not believable that each law enforcement officer can protect 360 to 450 people from violent criminals or answer every 911 call before the criminal fires a gun.

The sheer number of guns and gun owners in America makes gun control far more unrealistic than Prohibition. At least 80 million Americans own about 250 million guns, and about 99% of gun-owners obviously handle their guns responsibly or we would have many more accidents.

The marching moms say they want handguns registered and handgun owners licensed similarly to what is required for automobiles. But registering cars doesn't make kids any safer, and many other methods are obviously better at improving safety, such as safety instruction itself.

Using automobiles as an analogy doesn't help the marching moms' argument, anyway, because it invites us to put gun safety courses in schools like driver's ed.

It's time for Americans to separate truth from propaganda in news coverage about guns. Under the principle that "if it bleeds it leads," television redundantly reports on guns used to kill, but censors out the many incidents of successful defensive use of guns to disarm criminals and protect law-abiding citizens from becoming victims.

Guns are used to save lives almost five times as often as to commit crimes. Guns are used 430,000 times a year to commit crimes, but 2,000,000 to 2,500,000 times a year in self-defense to prevent deaths, rapes, assaults and other serious injuries. In 98% of the situations, the victim just brandished a gun, and in only 2% of the cases was the gun actually fired, usually just as a warning. But when was the last time you saw a news story about someone successfully using a gun in self-defense?

Gun control advocates refuse to make a risk-benefit analysis, balancing the good guns do against the harm. Instead, they use emotion and lies to plead their cause.

In the 31 states that have passed right-to-carry laws since the mid-1980s, the number of multiple-victim public shootings . . . has dropped dramatically.

All scientific studies show that restrictive gun laws are more dangerous than guns. Crime is reduced by putting guns in the hands of law-abiding citizens. Guns are the safest and most effective means of resisting violent criminal attack. Areas that increase gun ownership have lower crime rates than other areas. Even those who do not own a gun are safer because the criminal fears that his next victim might have the power to defend himself.

By definition, laws will be obeyed only by the law abiding. If we disarm those likely to obey the law, gun restrictions will encourage crime rather than prevent it. As Professor Lott warns: "Despite good intentions, gun-control advocates are going to end up risking more lives than they're going to save."

Why gun control does not work

"We need more gun regulations." False. There is no academic evidence that gun regulations prevent crime and plenty of evidence that they encourage crime. It stands to reason that, if we disarm those likely to obey the gun laws, we make crime more attractive, profitable and likely for those who do not obey the law. Washington, D.C. has the strictest gun control laws in the country and the highest murder rate, 69 per 100,000, while other major cities with more gun freedom have only a fraction of that rate. 200 scholars from major universities (Harvard, Stanford, Northwestern, UCLA) released an open letter to Congress on June 16, 1999 stating

that proposed new gun laws are ill-advised: "With the 20,000 gun laws already on the books, we advise Congress, before enacting yet more new laws, to investigate whether many of the existing laws may have contributed to the problems we currently face."

"The United States has a higher murder rate than other countries because Americans own so many guns." False. Switzerland and Israel have more gun ownership than the United States and their murder rate is far less. Switzerland has more guns per person than any country in the world, yet is one of the safest places to be. All males age 20 to 42 are required to keep fully automatic rifles or pistols at home. It's a common sight to see Israelis carrying sidearms. On the other hand, Brazil and Russia have complete gun control, and their murder rate is five times that of the United States.

The Brady waiting period has had no significant impact on murder or robbery rates.

"Guns in the home are so dangerous because most murders are acquaintance murders, that is, someone you know gets angry and picks up an available gun." False. The vast majority of "acquaintances" who kill involve drug dealers, gangs, prostitutes, cab drivers, barroom brawlers, etc., and 90% of murderers have criminal records.

"The easy availability of guns in the home contributes to crimes of passion and domestic violence." False. Denying guns denies a woman the ability to defend herself against an abusive man. Guns equalize the means of physical terror between men and women.

"Passive resistance is the safest response to an attacker." False. It depends on the means you have to resist. If a woman has only her fists to defend against a rapist, she's not likely to be successful with active resistance. But if the woman has a gun, active resistance can mean the difference between rape and safety.

The *"increase in rampage killings"* shows we need gun control. False again. Professor Lott, who did a couple of thousand hours of research on this issue, found that there has been no upward national trend in such killings since the mid-1970s.

"We need safe storage laws." False. States that passed "safe storage" laws have high crime rates, especially higher rates of rape and aggravated assault against women.

"We need waiting periods and background checks to reduce crime and youth violence." False. No academic study has shown that crime is reduced by waiting periods or background checks.

Clinton brags that we are safer because *"the Brady law has kept 500,000 criminals from buying handguns."* False. The only academic research done on the Brady law showed that the Brady waiting period has had no significant impact on murder or robbery rates and is associated with a small increase in rape and aggravated-assault rates, perhaps due to removing victims' ability to defend themselves.

"Guns create a terrible danger of accidental deaths." False. Rep. James Traficant (Democrat-Ohio) told the House: "Something does not add up, the number of accidental deaths involving guns average 1,500 per year;

and the number of accidental deaths caused by doctors, surgeons, and hospitals average 120,000 a year. That means . . . [it is] 80 times more possible of being killed accidentally by a doctor than a gun." (April 4, 2000)

"We should register guns and license gun owners just like automobiles, and that won't lead to confiscation because we haven't confiscated cars." That's a false analogy. There are 130 million automobiles in the United States weighing about a ton each and confiscation would be impossible. We've seen gun confiscation and its results in many other countries. The analogy to automobiles also fails because cars are not used in self-defense to protect lives.

"The gun show loophole must be closed." False. There is no gun show loophole. Anyone who is engaged in the business of selling firearms, whether at a gun show or a fixed retail store, must fill out a government registration form on every buyer and get FBI permission through the National Instant Check System for every sale. There is no evidence that gun shows are an important source of criminals' guns. A 1997 National Institute of Justice study in December 1997 reported that only 2% of felons acquired their guns at gun shows and those included purchases from licensed dealers who conducted background checks.

"Assault weapons should be banned." False. Civilian assault weapons are not machine guns. They are just ordinary guns that have a pseudo-military appearance. They do not fire faster, the bullets are not especially powerful, and they are slower than bullets from hunting rifles. Semi-automatic guns do not "spray" bullets and are not machine guns, they require a separate pull of the trigger for each shot to be fired just like a revolver. (Fully-automatic military assault rifles are *not* part of the current gun debate.)

"Handguns must be banned." False. The law abiding, by definition, will abide by the law; law violators will not. Handguns will always be available at some price; demand will create its own supply.

Gun confiscation leads to a loss of freedom, increased crime, and the government moving to the left.

"We must get rid of the Saturday Night Special." False. This is a small, low-caliber, short-barreled, not-too-expensive gun. Not only does this type of gun have a legitimate sports and recreational use, it is the best defensive weapon for poor, inner-city residents who are the most likely potential victims of crime. Why deny them protection?

"The American Society of Pediatrics says that handguns should be banned." But the pediatricians' statement is based on the usual bogus statistics, not on any scientific study. If the pediatricians did a scientific study, they might reach the same conclusion that Professor Lott did, namely, that more guns in the hands of law-abiding people result in less crime.

We are told that *"we need zero tolerance in the schools about guns."* But schools were a lot safer prior to the 1970s, when guns in schools were very common. Professor Lott has pointed out that, "until 1969, virtually every public high school in New York City had a shooting club. High school students carried their guns to school on the subways in the morning . . . and regularly competed in city-wide shooting contests." When guns were so easily accessible, even inside schools, why didn't we have the problems that we have today? The reason can't be that kids take guns to school.

Gun control in other nations

The chief reason America has remained a free country is the widespread private ownership of firearms. Individual ownership of guns made the American Revolution possible. The principal purpose of the Second Amendment was to maintain our freedom from government. It is an insult to our heritage to imply that the Founding Fathers wrote the Second Amendment just to protect deer hunters.

My good friend, the late Reverend Stephen Dunker, C.M., was a missionary in China who was imprisoned by the Communists during the early 1950s. I heard him tell of his experiences many times. When the Communists first took over the area where he lived, they appeared to be good rulers. They established law and order and cleaned up the traffic in drugs and prostitutes. Then one day the Communist bosses announced, "You can see that we have established a good society and you have no need for your guns. Everyone must come in the night and dump all guns in the town square." The people believed and obeyed. The next day, the reign of terror began, with public executions and cruel imprisonments. Everyone accused of being a "landlord" was dragged through the streets and executed; a "landlord" was anyone who farmed his little plot of ground with two water buffalo instead of one.

Gun confiscation leads to a loss of freedom, increased crime, and the government moving to the left. This has already happened in England and Australia. After Great Britain banned most guns in 1997, making armed self-defense punishable as murder, violence skyrocketed because criminals know that law abiding citizens have been disarmed. Armed crime rose 10% in 1998. The *Sunday Times* of London reported on the new black market in guns: "Up to 3 million illegal guns are in circulation in Britain, leading to a rise in drive-by shootings and gangland-style execution." There has been such a heavy increase in the use of knives for violent attacks that new laws have been passed giving police the power to search anyone for knives in designated areas.

In 1996 Australia banned 60% of all firearms and required registration of all guns and the licensing of gun owners. Police confiscated 640,381 firearms, going door to door without search warrants. Two years later, the Australian Bureau of Statistics reported that all crime had risen and armed robberies were up 44%.

Miguel A. Faria Jr., M.D., described his first-hand experience in Cuba. Before 1958, Cuban dictator Fulgencio Batista had all citizens register their firearms. After the revolution, Raul and Fidel Castro had their Communist thugs go door to door and, using the registration lists, confiscate all firearms. As soon as the Cubans were disarmed, that was the end of their freedom.

Tyrannical governments kill far more people than private criminals. The Nazis conducted a massive search-and-seizure operation in 1933 to disarm their political opponents, in 1938 to disarm the Jews, and when they occupied Europe in 1939–41 they proclaimed the death penalty for anyone who failed to surrender all guns within 24 hours.

The first line of safety has to be an ability to defend yourself. In some areas, a woman who is being stalked by her ex-husband must wait 10 days to buy a gun, even if her life has been threatened. Some cities criminalize carrying guns for self-defense but make exceptions for people carrying money or jewels. Are money and jewels more important to protect than people's lives?

History teaches us that registration leads to the confiscation of guns and that is the goal of many gun control advocates. Pete Shields, founder of Handgun Control Inc., told *The New Yorker*: "The first problem is to slow down the number of handguns being produced and sold in this country. The second problem is to get handguns registered. The final problem is to make possession of all handguns and all handgun ammunition—except for the military, police, licensed security guards, licensed sporting clubs, and licensed gun collectors—totally illegal."

Atlanta public-safety commissioner George Napper told *U.S. News*, "If I had my druthers, the only people who would have guns would be those who enforce the law." Like those who "enforced the law" at Waco? or at Ruby Ridge? or invading a Miami home to grab Elián Gonzalez?

Understanding the Second Amendment

The Second Amendment to the United States Constitution states: "A well regulated militia, being necessary to the security of a free state, the right of the people to keep and bear arms, shall not be infringed." Polls show that up to 80% of the public believe citizens have a constitutional right to own guns.

If the First Amendment read "A free press being necessary to the security of a free state, Congress shall make no law respecting . . . the freedom of speech, or of the press," nobody would argue that free speech belongs only to newspapers. Likewise, they should not argue that the right to keep and bear arms belongs only to government agents.

Chief Justice William Rehnquist, writing for the majority in *U.S. v. Verdugo-Urquidez* (1990), stated that the term "the people" has the same meaning in the First, Second, Fourth, Ninth and Tenth Amendments. All those five amendments in the Bill of Rights use the term "the people" to guarantee a right for individual citizens, not just some collective right of the state as a whole. There is no reason to believe that the Second Amendment uses the term "the people" differently from the other four amendments.

The claim that "militia" just refers to the National Guard is ridiculous. The same Congress that passed the Second Amendment also passed the Militia Act of 1792 which defined militia as "each and every able-bodied male citizen" from age 18 to 45 (with some exceptions), and stated that each one shall "provide himself" with a gun, ammunition, and a bayonet.

The currently effective Militia Act substantially keeps the same language ("all able-bodied males at least 17 years of age and . . . under 45"), and further defines militia as: "(1) the organized militia, which consists of the National Guard and the Naval Militia; and (2) the unorganized militia, which consists of the members of the militia who are not members of the National Guard or the Naval Militia." (10 U.S.C. 311)

In recent years, a scholarly consensus has emerged across the political spectrum that the Second Amendment protects an individual right. Between 1980 and 1995, of 39 law review articles, 35 noted the Supreme Court's prior acknowledgement of the individual right of the Second Amendment and only four claimed the right is a collective right of the states (and 3 of those 4 were authored or co-authored by persons connected with the gun-control lobby).

The Founding Fathers on the Right to Own Guns:

★ James Madison: Americans have "the advantage of being armed"— unlike the citizens of other countries where "the governments are afraid to trust the people with arms."

★ Patrick Henry: "The great objective is that every man be armed. . . . Everyone who is able may have a gun."

★ George Mason: "To disarm the people [is] the best and most effectual way to enslave them."

★ Samuel Adams: "The Constitution shall never be construed . . . to prevent the people of the United States who are peaceable citizens from keeping their own arms."

★ Alexander Hamilton: "The best we can hope for concerning the people at large is that they be properly armed."

★ Richard Henry Lee: "To preserve liberty, it is essential that the whole body of the people always possess arms, and be taught alike, especially when young, how to use them."

3

Gun Control Poses a Threat to Self-Defense

Robert J. Cottrol

Robert J. Cottrol is a professor of law and history at George Washington University in Washington, D.C. He is also the chair of the law and social science section of the Association of American Law Schools.

The Second Amendment gives Americans the right to own and carry guns. Gun control infringes on this right and limits people's ability to defend themselves. Gun control keeps guns out of the hands of the urban poor, the people who are most in need of self defense. Ironically, laws that allow people to carry concealed guns have been shown to reduce violent crime in minority communities. The dangers of limiting the right to self defense go beyond its effects in urban areas. When citizens lose the right to own guns, tyranny and genocide often follow, as has been shown by the actions of Hitler, Stalin, and Pol Pot.

> Certainly one of the chief guarantees of freedom under any government, no matter how popular and respected, is the right of the citizen to keep and bear arms. This is not to say that firearms should not be very carefully used and that definite rules of precaution should not be taught and enforced. But the right of the citizen to bear arms is just one more safeguard against a tyranny which now appears remote in America, but which historically has proved to be always possible.
>
> —Hubert Humphrey, 1960

M y background is probably atypical for a somewhat high-profile supporter of the right to keep and bear arms. I am black and grew up in Manhattan's East Harlem, far removed from the great American gun culture of rural, white America. Although my voting patterns have become somewhat more conservative in recent years, I remain in my heart of hearts a 1960s Humphrey Democrat concerned with the plight of those most vulnerable in American society—minorities, the poor, the elderly, and single women—groups whose day-to-day realities are often overlooked in our public policy debates, people whose lives too often go unnoticed by our intellectually timid chattering classes. This is happening in the public debate over the right to bear arms.

Attacks on the Second Amendment

For the nation's elites, the Second Amendment has become the Rodney Dangerfield of the Bill of Rights, constantly attacked by editorial writers, police chiefs seeking scapegoats, demagoging politicians, and even by Rosie O'Donnell, no less. It is threatened by opportunistic legislative efforts, even when sponsors acknowledge their proposed legislation would have little impact on crime and violence.

Professional champions of civil rights and civil liberties have been unwilling to defend the underlying principle of the right to arms. Even the conservative defense has been timid and often inept, tied less, one suspects, to abiding principle and more to the dynamics of contemporary Republican politics. Thus a right older than the Republic, one that the drafters of two constitutional amendments—the Second and the Fourteenth—intended to protect, and a right whose critical importance has been painfully revealed by twentieth-century history, is left undefended by the lawyers, writers, and scholars we routinely expect to defend other constitutional rights. Instead, the Second Amendment's intellectual as well as political defense has been left in the unlikely hands of the National Rifle Association (NRA). And although the NRA deserves considerably better than the demonized reputation it has acquired, it should not be the sole or even principal voice in defense of a major constitutional provision.

This anemic defense is all the more embarrassing because it occurs as mounting evidence severely undermines the three propositions that have been central to the anti-gun movement since its appearance on the national radar screen in the 1960s. The first proposition is that the Constitution, particularly the Second Amendment, poses no barrier to radical gun control, even total prohibition of private firearms. The second is that ordinary citizens with firearms are unlikely to defend themselves and are more likely to harm innocent parties with their guns. The final proposition is that the case for radical gun control is buttressed by comparing the United States to nations with more restrictive firearms policies. These propositions, now conventional wisdom, simply do not stand up to scrutiny.

The proposition that the Second Amendment poses no barrier to gun prohibition—a claim largely unknown before the 1960s—has run up against stubborn, contrary historical facts. Increasingly, historians and legal scholars, including many who support stricter gun control, have examined the history of the Second Amendment, the development of the right to arms in English political thought, judicial commentaries on the right in antebellum America, and the debates over the Fourteenth Amendment. The consensus among scholars who have actually looked at the evidence is that the Second and Fourteenth Amendments were meant to protect the citizen's right to arms. (See, for example, historian Joyce Lee Malcolm's Harvard University Press book, *To Keep and Bear Arms*, or the historical documents assembled in the three *Gun Control and the Constitution* volumes I've edited.)

Similarly, the criminological premises of the anti-gun movement have collapsed in the face of serious social science. For better than three decades the American public has been solemnly assured that peaceable citizens who possess guns for self-defense are disasters in waiting. "A gun in the home is more likely to kill a member of the family than to defend against an intruder," we hear. "Allowing citizens to carry firearms outside the home for self-protection will turn our streets into Dodge City and our parking lots into the O.K. Corral," the refrain goes.

Yet the criminological literature provides little support for this caricature of gun owners. Instead, careful research has discovered an incredibly high amount of firearms being responsibly used in self-defense. Research by Florida State University criminologist Gary Kleck and others indicate between two and three million cases of self-defense per year. Overwhelmingly these incidents involve *not* firing the weapon at the attacker, but simply brandishing it and thereby causing the attacker's withdrawal.

Over 1 million Americans have licenses to carry firearms, but firearms misuse by this group has been utterly negligible.

In recent years a majority of states have passed laws permitting honest citizens to carry concealed weapons, and the results tell us much about self-defense and the responsibility of the average citizen. Once it was passionately argued that such laws would turn minor altercations into bloody shoot-outs; now we know better. Over 1 million Americans have licenses to carry firearms, but firearms misuse by this group has been utterly negligible. Criminologists now debate not how much harm has been caused by concealed-carry laws, but how much good.

The most thorough research, by John Lott of the University of Chicago, reveals that concealed-carry laws have had a substantial deterrent effect on crimes of violence. His work shows that women, especially, have benefitted, as substantial drops in rapes and attacks on women have occurred where the laws have been enacted. Lott also discovered dramatic benefits for the urban poor and minorities: "Not only do urban areas tend to gain in their fight against crime, but reductions in crime rates are greatest precisely in those urban areas that have the highest crime rates, largest and most dense populations, and greatest concentrations of minorities."

Comparing gun control

The final proposition—that international comparisons prove the case for radical gun control—may be the most problematic of all. Certainly the simplistic conclusion that American homicide rates are higher than those in Western Europe and Japan because of the greater prevalence of firearms glosses over significant cultural and demographic differences between us and other advanced industrial nations.

The American population is younger and more diverse. Unlike Western Europe and Japan, the United States has always had a large number of immigrants and internal migrants. We also have a history of racial exclusion and a struggle against that exclusion as old as the Republic and without real parallel in comparable nations. All of these have contributed to crime rates higher than those in other western nations. Indeed, when a number of the cultural and demographic variables are controlled for, much of the apparent difference between American and Western European homicide rates disappears—despite the greater presence of firearms in American society.

Protection against tyranny

But international comparisons should raise deeper and more disturbing questions, questions too rarely asked in serious company. The central and usually unchallenged premise of the gun control movement is that society becomes more civilized when the citizen surrenders the means of self-defense, leaving the state a monopoly of force.

That this premise goes largely unchallenged is the most remarkable feature of our gun control debate. We are ending a century that has repeatedly witnessed the consequences of unchecked state monopolies of force. University of Hawaii political scientist Rudolph J. Rummel, one of the leading students of democide (mass murder of civilian populations by governments), has estimated that nearly 170 million people have been murdered by their own governments in our century. The familiar list of mass murderers—Hitler, Stalin, Mao, Pol Pot—only scratches the surface. The mass slaughter of helpless, unarmed civilian populations continues to this very day in Sudan, Rwanda, and parts of the former Yugoslavia.

The reluctance of outside forces to intervene is well documented. And yet the obvious question is strangely absent: Would arms in the hands of average citizens have made a difference? Could the overstretched Nazi war machine have murdered 11 million armed and resisting Europeans while also taking on the Soviet and Anglo-American armies? Could 50,000–70,000 Khmer Rouge have butchered 2–3 million armed Cambodians? These questions bear repeating. The answers are by no means clear, but it is unconscionable they are not being asked.

The constant effort to ban pistols poor people can afford . . . den[ies] the means of self-defense to entire communities.

Need Americans have such concerns? Well, we have been spared rule by dictators, but state tyranny can come in other forms. It can come when government refuses to protect unpopular groups—people who are disfavored because of their political or religious beliefs, or their ancestry, or the color of their skin. Our past has certainly not been free of this brand of state tyranny. In the Jim Crow South, for example, government failed and indeed refused to protect blacks from extra-legal violence. Given our history, it's stunning we fail to question those who would force upon us a total reliance on the state for defense.

Nor should our discussion of freedom and the right to arms be limited to foreign or historical examples. The lives and freedoms of decent, law-abiding citizens throughout our nation, especially in our dangerous inner cities, are constantly threatened by criminal predators. This has devastated minority communities. And yet the effort to limit the right to armed self-defense has been most intense in such communities. Bans on firearms ownership in public housing, the constant effort to ban pistols poor people can afford—scornfully labeled "Saturday Night Specials" and more recently "junk guns"—are denying the means of self-defense to entire communities in a failed attempt to disarm criminal predators. In too many communities, particularly under-protected minority communities, citizens have simply been disarmed and left to the mercy of well-armed criminals.

This has led to further curtailment of freedom. Consider initiatives in recent years to require tenants in public housing to allow their apartments to be searched: First, police failed for decades, for justifiable but also far too frequently unjustifiable reasons, to protect citizens in many of our most dangerous public housing projects. Next, as the situation became sufficiently desperate, tenants were prohibited from owning firearms for their own defense. Finally the demand came, "Surrender your right to privacy in your home." The message could not be clearer: A people incapable of protecting themselves will lose their rights as a free people, becoming either servile dependents of the state or of the criminal predators who are their *de facto* masters.

Freedom and the Second Amendment

All of this should force us to reconsider our debate over arms and rights. For too long, it has been framed as a question of the rights of sportsmen. It is far more serious: The Second Amendment has something critical to say about the relationship between the citizen and the state. For most of human history, in most of the nations in the world, the individual has all too often been a helpless dependent of the state, beholden to the state's benevolence and indeed competence for his physical survival.

The notion of a right to arms bespeaks a very different relationship. It says the individual is not simply a helpless bystander in the difficult and dangerous task of ensuring his or her safety. Instead, the citizen is an active participant, an equal partner with the state in ensuring not only his own safety but that of his community.

This is a serious right for serious people. It takes the individual from servile dependency on the state to the status of participating citizen, capable of making intelligent choices in defense of one's life and ultimately one's freedom. This conception of citizenship recognizes that the ultimate civil right is the right to defend one's own life, that without that right all other rights are meaningless, and that without the *means* of self-defense the right to self-defense is but an empty promise.

Our serious thinkers have been absent from this debate for too long. The Second Amendment is simply too important to leave to the gun nuts.

4

Compromising on Gun Control Can Reduce Gun Violence

Gary Rosen

Gary Rosen is the managing editor for the monthly magazine Commentary *and the author of* American Compact: James Madison and the Problem of Founding.

A middle ground needs to be reached on gun control. Such a compromise is necessary because both sides of the issue have valid arguments. Supporters of gun control point out the inadequacies of current laws in preventing the high rates of firearm fatalities. However, opponents of gun control have correctly argued that legislation has little effect on adolescent gun-related deaths and mass shootings. Although opponents have also shown that gun ownership can be a deterrent to crime, they have too readily opposed necessary measures, such as restrictions on assault weapons. A common sense approach to gun laws would include a background check for private transactions and improving the instant check system.

Gun control is hardly a new issue in American politics, but its current prominence—with the presidential candidates staking out positions on such esoteric matters as trigger locks and the "gunshow loophole"—would seem to require some explaining. After all, the U.S. continues to enjoy an unprecedented downturn in the crime rate. For eight consecutive years and across every major category of crime, the country has grown considerably safer, with the most impressive gains coming in urban areas. In New York City, to take just one much-celebrated example, the incidence of rape has dropped by 35 percent, aggravated assault by 37 percent, and robbery by 62 percent; having suffered some 2,200 murders as recently as 1990, the city recorded fewer than 700 in each of the last two years. What such statistics fail to register, of course, is the shock and outrage caused throughout the country by one small subset of violent crimes: the mass shootings that have recently occurred with bloody regularity in corners of American life usually spared such things.

[In 1999] alone, there were highly publicized attacks at a brokerage firm in Atlanta, a Jewish community center in Los Angeles, and a church in Fort Worth. Still more disturbing have been the more than a half-dozen episodes since 1997 in which students have opened fire at their own schools, the deadliest of these assaults being the one at Columbine High School in Littleton, Colorado, where two teenage gunmen killed twelve of their classmates and a teacher before taking their own lives. As the number of these shootings has mounted, so, too, has public concern. How have such young, or deranged, or racist malefactors been able to acquire the lethal instruments of their rage?

For the proponents of gun control, the answer is simple: the country is awash in firearms, and, thanks to the obstructionism of the National Rifle Association (NRA) and its political allies, we have not done nearly enough to keep weapons out of the hands of the most dangerous members of society. Moreover, they add, for all the recent progress in fighting crime, the U.S. remains the most violent of Western societies, with a death toll from gun-related incidents vastly exceeding that of nations with more stringent regulations and fewer firearms. What the country thus desperately needs, it is said—in the joint rallying cry of [spring 2000's] "Million Mom March," of advocacy groups like Handgun Control, Inc. (HCI), and of a swelling chorus of sympathetic politicians and editorialists—is a full range of "sensible" or "common sense" gun laws.

Changing trends in gun ownership

Ownership of guns is extraordinarily widespread in the United States, and has been for some time. Indeed, since the late 1950's, when surveys on this question were first done, the share of American households reporting at least one firearm has remained fairly constant at just under 50 percent. Needless to say, this does not mean that there is a gun-owner behind every second door in any American community. Guns are much more common in the Rocky Mountain states, South, and Midwest; in every region of the country, they are most likely to belong to middle-class, middle-aged men who live in rural areas or small towns. A useful shorthand for all this demography is that the average American gun-owner, both today and in the past, has tended to be a hunter or target-shooter.

What has changed dramatically over the last several decades is the size and composition of the American gun stock. The total number of firearms in circulation across the country has expanded at an astonishing rate, from about 75 million in the late 1960's to some 230 million today. At the same time, and despite the continuing predominance of the "long" guns (that is, rifles and shotguns) favored by sportsmen, an ever-increasing share of these firearms has consisted of handguns, whose primary use, as the supporters of stricter controls like to say, is against people. Such weapons have proliferated both among criminals, who use them in more than four out of five gun-related crimes, and among law-abiding citizens, especially urbanites, concerned about self-protection. As a result of these trends, Americans are now thought to possess somewhere in the neighborhood of 80 million handguns.

This shift in the character of ownership has taken place against a complicated legal backdrop, the basic feature of which at the federal level is the Gun Control Act of 1968. Passed in the aftermath of a spate of inner-city riots and the assassinations of Martin Luther King, Jr. and Robert Kennedy, the act was something of a catch-all, its provisions ranging from restrictions on machine guns to new federal penalties for the criminal use of a firearm. Its central aim, however, was to establish, for the first time, certain national standards concerning how guns are sold, and to whom. Dealers were required to obtain a federal license, to keep records of their sales (including the serial numbers newly mandated for all guns), to limit their interstate business, and to put an end to mail-order deliveries. More importantly, they were obliged to refuse guns to minors and to several categories of people now prohibited by federal law from possessing them, including convicted felons, fugitives from justice, drug abusers, and anyone with a history of serious mental illness.

The chief addition to this original set of federal controls has been the Brady Act, which went into effect in 1994. Named for James Brady, the White House press secretary gravely wounded in the attempt on President Reagan's life in 1981, the law requires licensed dealers to run a background check on prospective buyers, who previously had only to sign a form declaring that they did not fall into any of the prohibited groups. To make such investigations more practical—and less onerous for purchasers—the legislation also created a computerized "national instant check system" for criminal records. Under the supervision of the FBI, this system has been in operation since 1998.[1]

Far outnumbering federal regulations are the various local and state laws that have long been the principal source of firearms control in the U.S. As one might expect, these vary widely, according to the political tendencies and "gun culture" of different parts of the country. Even before passage of the Brady Act, about half the states, but especially more urbanized ones with higher crime rates, were already conducting background checks on purchasers, usually as part of a state-run system of licensing or registration. A few states also ban an assortment of semiautomatic "assault" weapons (thus supplementing a less comprehensive federal ban), and others have passed "child-access-prevention" laws, making it a crime to leave a gun within easy reach of a juvenile.

But where the states diverge most among themselves is in their treatment of handguns. Several have set a limit of just one purchase a month or have outlawed the cheap, smaller guns popularly known as "Saturday-night specials," and a substantial minority impose a waiting period of their own, typically seven days or less, before a sale may be completed. A number of localities, including New York City, Chicago, and Washington, D.C., have gone still farther, passing ordinances that are so restrictive as to make the legal acquisition of a handgun virtually impossible. In most of the country, however, such firearms are essentially available on demand to any federally qualified buyer. In addition, more than 30 states, from Oregon to Florida to Maine, allow anyone who meets certain basic

---

(1) In the four years before the "instant" system was available, the Brady Act provided a waiting period of up to five days for the completion of a background check and applied exclusively to handguns; it now covers all firearms bought from a licensed dealer.

requirements to receive a concealed-handgun permit, entitling its holder to keep a weapon at the ready in a holster, pocket, or purse; the legislation giving Texans this right was signed into law in 1995 by Governor George W. Bush.

A call for new laws

To the critics of this patchwork regime of local, state, and federal laws, its gross inadequacy is best seen in the high number of lives regularly lost to firearms in the U.S. Thanks to the "nation's porous gun laws," the *New York Times* declared in an editorial, "more than 80 Americans, including about a dozen children, continue to die every day from gun violence." For Handgun Control, Inc., the largest and most influential of the gun-control lobbies, the cumulative figures from this carnage suggest a damning analogy. "In 1997, 32,436 Americans were killed with firearms," the group notes. "In comparison, 33,651 Americans were killed in the Korean war, and 58,148 Americans were killed in the Vietnam war."

What is perhaps surprising about these gun fatalities is how few of them, relatively speaking, are the result of homicide. As HCI and its sister organizations emphasize, firearms pose a threat to "public health" that extends well beyond their role in the commission of violent crimes. Of the deaths in HCI's alarming tally, almost 13,000 were murders—but some 17,500 were suicides and nearly 1,000 were accidents. "The nexus is inescapable," according to an analyst for the Violence Policy Center. "The more accessibility to guns you have, the higher the rates of gun-related death and injury."

The total number of firearms in circulation across the country has expanded at an astonishing rate.

The senselessness of this human destruction is compounded, in the eyes of gun-control advocates, by the fundamental delusion that persuades so many Americans to own firearms in the first place. "It is important to remember that the belief that handguns are useful for self-defense is misguided," warns the Coalition to Stop Gun Violence, reporting an oft-cited study's conclusion that "a firearm in the home is 43 times more likely to be used for suicide or murder than self-defense." Worse, because so many guns kept in the home are stored recklessly or lack safety features, children have frequently been their special victims, inadvertently doing grievous harm to themselves and others. As HCI starkly puts it, presumably with a view to the suburbanites who are among its prime supporters, American parents have too often dropped off a child "at a friend's house for an afternoon play session or a sleep-over party not knowing that the car ride would be the last time they would see their child alive."

For the proponents of gun control, any solution to America's gun problem must be, like the problem itself, national in scope. Left to their own devices—and to the grassroots machinations of the NRA—too many states, they argue, have failed to pass adequate regulations, thereby endangering not just their own citizens but those of other states as well.

One broad set of remedies proposed in recent years—and pursued both on Capitol Hill and through lawsuits against the firearms industry—has focused on design and manufacture. Under these supply-side measures, gun-makers would be required, among other things, to stop producing "Saturday-night specials" and to add various safety features to their other handguns, from trigger locks meant for the protection of children to "smart" technology that, when fully developed, would allow a weapon to be fired only by an authorized user.

As for the demand side of the equation, gun-control groups have called for new laws that would place further barriers in the path of criminals and other people prohibited from buying firearms. At the top of this list, particularly after investigators discovered where the weapons used in the Columbine massacre were obtained, has been closing the "gun-show loophole." As matters now stand at such events (more than 4,000 of which are held each year), private collectors and hobbyists—unlike the licensed gun dealers who set up their wares alongside them—do not have to run background checks on potential buyers, and as a result, critics contend, they have become a key source for criminals and the illegal gun trade.

Much more ambitious, if less of-the-moment politically, is the idea of a national system of registration and licensing. The most fully articulated plan of this sort, a bill introduced in the Senate to coincide with the Million Mom March, would require anyone selling a handgun or semiautomatic firearm, whether a dealer or a private citizen, to provide the government with a record of sale, including a serial number. In addition, anyone wishing to buy such guns—or anyone owning older versions of them—would have to obtain a federal firearms license, a process that would include an extensive background check, a written safety test, and a thumbprint. Such a system, a spokesman for HCI told the *Atlanta Journal and Constitution*, "would make sure that the wrong people don't get a hold of guns; make sure that people know how to use guns properly; [and] make it easier for police to trace crime guns and detect gun traffickers."

A closer look at gun violence

That those urging the adoption of these laws would present them as simple expressions of "common sense" is understandable. There is no denying the large number of Americans killed by gunfire each year. More to the point, there seems to be something obvious, even self-evident, in the idea that the general availability of guns goes a long way toward explaining the country's high rates of violence, or that placing further limits on manufacturers, dealers, and owners would help to save lives.

Commonplace as these intuitions may be, however, and central though they are to the abiding popular appeal of gun control, they deserve scrutiny—at least if the ultimate objective is indeed a truly "sensible" set of policies. A useful place to begin is with the "firearm facts" routinely deployed by the advocates of gun control. These, as it happens, are frequently either incomplete or misleading, and especially so with respect to children, whose vulnerability to random gun violence has been grossly exaggerated in order to score political points.

Of the "dozen children" killed by guns each day, for example, about ten are older adolescents, aged fifteen to nineteen, and most of them perish as a result of involvement in drug or gang activity.[2] Preteen children, by contrast, are rarely the victims of fatal gun accidents, the overall incidence of which has been dropping steadily for decades. Although trigger locks and "child-access-prevention" laws may avert a few of these domestic tragedies (and are arguably worthwhile for that reason), as accident risks go, particularly among the children solicitously delivered to "afternoon play sessions" and "sleep-over parties," backyard swimming pools should be a much greater cause for concern: despite being present in far fewer households than are guns, they take many times the number of young lives.

As for suicide, there is no reason to think that its likelihood is higher because of the widespread availability of firearms. To the contrary, despite a three-fold increase in the number of guns in the U.S. over the last three decades, the total suicide rate has remained fairly constant. Gun suicides have occurred slightly more often—they now account for over half the firearm deaths in the country—but when guns are less readily to hand, people who are determined to kill themselves just resort to other equally lethal means.

Firearms pose a threat to "public health" that extends well beyond their role in the commission of violent crimes.

Much the same logic applies to the acts of criminal violence that are most troubling to the public and to policy-makers. As recent history demonstrates—with gun ownership on a steep rise while rates of murder, robbery, and assault have dropped precipitously—the total volume of violent crime in the U.S. is unconnected to the prevalence of guns in American society at large. Guns certainly make such violence as we have more deadly, but they in no sense generate that violence, and still less do they explain the dispiriting fact that we murder one another much more often than do Europeans or the Japanese. Alas, we do so in every category of homicide, whether the instrument is a gun, a knife, or a fist. Instructive too in this regard is a comparison to countries like Switzerland, Norway, and Israel, where household gun ownership is very common but violent crime is not.

Considerable modesty is also in order when it comes to the utility of gun laws for preventing further mass shootings. "No more Columbines" may be a rousing slogan, but the perpetrators of the Columbine massacre—like their counterparts in a number of similar incidents—would not have been stopped by the new regulations that have been proposed. Although it is true that the guns used in the Colorado attack were bought from private collectors at gun shows and that neither of the "straw" purchasers who obtained them for the killers underwent a background check, had

(2) Even the figure of a "dozen," based on data from 1997, is no longer accurate; statistics released in July by the federal Centers for Disease Control and Prevention put the daily toll of "children" at ten for 1998, continuing the downward trend of recent years.

they been required to do so, both would have been approved, their records having been completely clean.

Or consider the case of Larry Gene Ashbrook, the forty-seven-year-old loner who killed seven people, including four teenagers, at a Fort Worth church [in September 1999]. Though irascible and mentally unbalanced according to neighbors and police, he had never committed a felony or undergone psychiatric treatment, and was in no way barred by law from buying the pistol used in his murderous rampage. If a federal license had been necessary for this purchase, he would have had no trouble qualifying for one. As *Newsweek* commented at the time—and as one can say of mass shootings in general, considering how utterly atypical they are among gun murders—"the hard lesson of Ashbrook's spree was that there are some dangers against which society might just not have a clear defense."

The total volume of violent crime in the U.S. is unconnected to the prevalence of guns in American society at large.

Finally, there is the issue of self-protection, perhaps the most important in the entire gun-control debate and the one concerning which proponents of gun control tend to be at their most disingenuous. As Iain Murray of the nonprofit Statistical Assessment Service observes, the endlessly repeated claim—or some variation of it—that "a firearm in the home is 43 times more likely to be used for suicide or murder than self-defense" has been "discredited completely," for it depends "on the very rare instance of someone actually shooting dead, as opposed to scaring off or wounding, an intruder." When the defensive use of firearms is defined more reasonably to include, in particular, its most common form, which is the simple display of a gun, the picture that emerges is radically different.

The most comprehensive research on this issue, conducted by the criminologist Gary Kleck of Florida State University, suggests that Americans use guns to ward off a criminal aggressor as many as 2.5 million times a year—a figure roughly three times higher, Kleck points out, than the number of gun-related crimes committed each year. Far from being foolhardy or dangerous, as skeptics contend, such resistance makes it less likely that would-be victims will lose their property in a robbery or be injured in an assault. Surveys of imprisoned felons confirm that the possibility of confronting an armed victim is among their biggest worries.

A narrower, if more provocative, case for the deterrent effect of private gun ownership has been made by John R. Lott, Jr., a research scholar at Yale Law School. In his much-discussed 1998 book, *More Guns, Less Crime*,([3]) Lott analyzed the state laws allowing most citizens to qualify for a concealed-handgun permit—a privilege that gun-control advocates have derided, and fought, as a sure recipe for Wild-West-style shootouts. Not only, he found, have such "right-to-carry" laws failed to spark irresponsible gun use, but they have driven down rates of violence, with the

---

(3) It has recently been reissued in an updated paperback edition: University of Chicago Press, 321 pp., $12.00.

most dramatic progress often occurring in those urban jurisdictions, like Pittsburgh and Atlanta, that saw the largest increase in the number of permits issued. Lott's conclusion: the carrying of concealed handguns is "the most cost-effective means of reducing crime."

Examining the views of the gun lobby

Does all this mean that the opponents of gun control and in particular the NRA are right? To some extent, it does. Despite their often incendiary rhetoric—"From my cold, dead hands!" intoned NRA president Charlton Heston, hoisting a musket over his head at the group's annual convention in May [2000]—they do keep the national debate honest. This is not because they are necessarily honest themselves, but because the view they espouse is so intransigently at odds with the anti-gun prejudices of the country's educated elite and major media organs. With close to 4 million members, the NRA is a standing reminder that, however distasteful firearms may be considered in Manhattan or Georgetown or Beverly Hills, a great many ordinary Americans own and value them for a range of perfectly valid reasons.

It is therefore all the more unfortunate that these legitimate interests have been translated, as a practical matter, into a virtually absolutist rejection of any proposal for the regulation of firearms. The usual starting point for the NRA is the Second Amendment, which declares, in its much-fought-over 27 words, "A well-regulated militia, being necessary to the security of a free state, the right of the people to keep and bear arms, shall not be infringed." For advocates of gun control, the amendment's introductory phrases about the militia render it little more than an 18th-century curiosity, a constitutional anachronism best left to historians of the early republic. For the NRA and its sympathizers, it is the main clause that counts, describing in unequivocal language an individual right no less fundamental than those enshrined in the First Amendment.

But even if this latter view is basically correct—and I believe that it is—it is a far cry from a general prohibition on laws regulating the sale and ownership of firearms. Short of banning most guns or denying them to certain individuals without cause—measures that would strike at the core right "to keep and bear arms"—the government would seem to have a substantial degree of latitude under the Second Amendment. As the legal scholar Nelson Lund recently wrote in the *Weekly Standard*, urging the courts to take this part of the Bill of Rights more seriously, "most existing federal regulations . . . would probably survive such scrutiny because they are sufficiently well tailored to achieve sufficiently important government purposes."

As for the many specific measures that the gun lobby has invariably resisted over the years, some have been worth combating and others have not. There is, for instance, every reason to oppose efforts (like that of Vice President Gore) to ban "Saturday-night specials." Though criminals show no special preference for these small, inexpensive guns, they are often the only ones that the law-abiding poor can afford for self-defense. It is worth noting in this connection that the idea of singling out such weapons originated in the Jim Crow South as a means of disarming blacks; the name for them comes from the racist epithet, "nigger-town Saturday night."

Similarly, the imposition of costly "smart-gun" technology on firearms manufacturers would have the effect—if it should ever get off the drawing board—of pricing many low-income people out of the market.

What of restrictions on machine guns and "assault" weapons, plastic guns and armor-piercing bullets? It is here that the supporters of gun rights have displayed an astonishing and self-destructive obtuseness, even as they have sometimes acceded to such measures under political duress. Their argument that these weapons and munitions are seldom used in crime (which is in fact the case) is quite beside the point. Such menacing firearms are widely, and rightly, viewed as falling outside any reasonable recreational or protective need—as HCI asks, "Who needs an AK-47 to go duck-hunting?"—and the simple prospect of their availability is perceived as a threat to public safety. Even if the stakes involved are largely symbolic, symbols matter.

There are problems, too, with what is perhaps the most formidable argument of the gun lobby: that gun control is pointless because, in the words of one NRA brochure, "criminals do not bother with the niceties of obeying laws—for a criminal is, by definition, someone who disobeys laws." This is certainly true, but not in an unqualified sense. Gary Kleck, whose *Targeting Guns* (1997)[4] is an encyclopedic scholarly critique of the key assumptions of gun control, agrees that "many criminals will ignore gun laws and get guns anyway." But as he notes, this is hardly "decisive regarding the desirability of gun control, since it does not address the number of successes of gun control. . . . It is even conceivable that if just 1 or 2 percent of potentially violent persons could be denied a gun, the resulting benefits might exceed the costs of whatever measure produced this modest level of compliance." The question, then, is how this calculus plays out with a given policy.

The benefits of background checks

For the system of background checks that is now the centerpiece of federal gun-control law, the benefits are not difficult to see. In 1999, according to the Justice Department, more than 200,000 gun-sale applications were rejected because the buyer was disqualified in some way, overwhelmingly for a felony conviction or indictment. Since the Brady Act went into effect in 1994, such rejections have numbered well over a half-million. It is true that a small fraction of these, especially early on, resulted from bureaucratic foul-ups. Moreover, the fact that individuals with a criminal record were unable to get a gun from a licensed dealer tells us nothing about whether they were ultimately able to get a gun, a problem highlighted by a widely reported study of the Brady Act published [in August 2000] in the *Journal of the American Medical Association*. Still, for the price of making everyone submit to a slight administrative inconvenience, hundreds of thousands of high-risk bad guys have been denied weapons at the moment they wanted them.

Should the requirement of running background checks apply to the hobbyists and collectors who set up shop at gun shows? Those opposed to the notion point with some justice to its arbitrariness, since it would not affect the private sale of firearms at any other venue: to skirt the new

(4) Aldine de Gruyter, 450 pp., $26.95 (paperback)

law, private sellers could just arrange to complete their transactions else-where. But such critics draw the wrong conclusion. What the "gun-show loophole" really illustrates is the need to extend the terms of the Brady Act to every private transfer of a firearm, whether at a gun show or not.

Gun-owners would squawk, but the requirement would not be espe-cially burdensome. It would merely mean having to use a licensed dealer as a broker for private firearms transactions—of which there are some 3 million each year—in order to ensure a proper background check. The arrangement already prevails on the Internet, where sales of guns—as of everything else—have grown exponentially in recent years. Would many people evade this system? Certainly. But enough would make a good-faith effort at compliance to hinder the immediate acquisition of fire-arms by criminals, who are much more likely to get their guns in a pri-vate exchange—or from theft—than from a licensed dealer.

> *Neither side is right [about gun violence], but, at this particular juncture, it is . . . the devotees of gun control that [stand] to do more harm.*

An even more promising way to keep firearms from falling into dan-gerous hands, it is said, would be a federal system for registering guns and licensing gun-owners. This idea is supported, according to opinion polls, by a sizable majority of Americans. The NRA, however, is vehemently op-posed, seeing registration in particular as the first bureaucratic step to-ward the eventual banning of firearms, as indeed it was in the de-facto prohibition of handguns now in effect in Washington, D.C., and Chicago. But the more serious objection to any national scheme of regis-tration is of an opposite complexion: not that it would be too irresistibly efficient but that it would be almost completely irrelevant. As even the rather visionary proposal introduced in the Senate concedes in its details, no viable system of registration could apply retroactively—that is, to ex-isting firearms; the expense and administrative complications would be too great, not to mention the political grief of persuading (or compelling) current gun-owners to cooperate. What this means is that, under the bill, registration would apply, at most, to the 5 or 6 million handguns and semiautomatic weapons that are sold new or privately transferred each year—leaving the rest of America's 230 million guns untouched. Such limited information may be worth having in order to discourage illicit sales, but even decades from now it would make a negligible difference in solving all but a tiny handful of gun crimes.

As for insisting that every gun-owner obtain a federal license, there is again the question of efficacy. The research that has been done on li-censing, as well as on waiting periods, suggests that whatever impact these measures have on reducing violent crime is owed to the background checks that they entail. If such checks are expanded, as they should be, to cover all gun transactions, licensing would merely duplicate the effort. A better use of time and money would be to improve the accuracy and ac-cessibility of both the FBI's "national instant check system" and the sim-ilar screening operations run by many of the states.

Reaching a consensus

"Common sense," in short, should indeed be our guide in devising gun laws, but its dictates are not as clear as the advocates of further regulations would have us believe. Banning whole categories of firearms amounts at most to a reassuring gesture (as with "assault" weapons) but can also interfere with the legitimate right of self-defense (as with "Saturday-night specials"). Safety measures like trigger locks may save a few lives on the margins, but allowing law-abiding citizens to carry handguns may do even more in this regard. And background checks are a helpful tool—but they are only that, not a solution for the "gun problem," whose dimensions, in any event, have little to do with our society's possessing so very many firearms.

It has often been observed that, though generally well disposed to gun control, the American public doubts such laws will have much of an effect on stopping crime. Far from being contradictory, this view strikes a nice balance, reflecting as it does not only the reasonable belief that having some effect on stopping crime is no bad thing but also a realistic assessment of the result of most gun regulations.

Arrayed on either side of this sober consensus, however, are the true believers, the noisiest participants in what B. Bruce-Briggs, writing in the *Public Interest* in the mid-1970's, could even then call "the great American gun war." The NRA plays its part, defending a nearly unconditional right "to keep and bear arms." On the other side, HCI, the "Million Moms," and the *New York Times* play theirs, waving a bloody banner after each new outburst of gun violence and declaring "if only there had been a law." Neither side is right, but, at this particular juncture, it is the latter group, the devotees of gun control, that stands to do more harm.

This is not because the gun controllers will see their agenda fully realized, but rather because their extravagant rhetoric, magnified by the powerful forums available to them, has begun to shift the terms of a more fundamental debate, the one over crime, in an ominous direction, away from the strategies that have made the U.S. so demonstrably safer a place in recent years. For those who have never been happy with aggressive policing, or high incarceration rates, gun control has become a useful diversion, explicitly targeting a colorful array of "rednecks" and "gun nuts" but implicitly placing under moral suspicion anyone who owns or uses a firearm. To the degree that this hysteria over guns causes the rest of us, including public officials and the police, to lose sight of the real crime problem—and the criminals behind it—it is a dangerous and deeply worrisome development.

5

Concealed-Carry Laws Reduce Violent Crime

John R. Lott Jr.

John R. Lott Jr., the author of More Guns, Less Crime, *is the John M. Olin Law and Economics Fellow at the University of Chicago Law School.*

Concealed-carry laws allow law-abiding citizens to carry concealed handguns. Concealed handguns reduce violent crime by making it easier for citizens to defend themselves. Concealed-carry laws benefit society as a whole, not just the citizens that are armed, because a criminal is less likely to attack if he or she thinks the potential victim could be carrying a gun. Such laws have been shown to significantly reduce the number of murders, rapes, assaults, and robberies. Permitting concealed handguns would not lead to shootings at traffic accidents or greatly increase incidents of accidental shootings as opponents claim. Preventing citizens from carrying guns does not make them secure from violence but increases their vulnerability to it.

To gun control advocates, the logic of opposing concealed handgun laws is straightforward. If guns are introduced into a violent encounter, the probability that someone will die increases. Murders are viewed as arising from unintentional fits of rage that are quickly regretted, and simply keeping guns out of people's reach will prevent deaths. More guns are also seen as leading to more accidental gun deaths. The solution is clear: more regulation or even the complete elimination of guns.

Those who advocate letting law-abiding citizens carry concealed handguns point to polls of American citizens undertaken by organizations like the *Los Angeles Times* and Gallup showing that Americans defend themselves with guns between 764,000 and 3.6 million times each year, with the vast majority of cases simply involving people brandishing a gun to prevent attack.[1] Victims (such as women or the elderly) are most often much weaker than the criminals that attack them. Guns are seen by these advocates as the great equalizer, and allowing concealed handguns provides citizens even greater ability to defend themselves.

While cases like the 1992 incident in which a Japanese student was shot on his way to a Halloween party in Louisiana make international headlines,[2] they are rare. In another highly publicized case, a Dallas resident recently became the only Texas resident so far charged with using a permitted concealed weapon in a fatal shooting.[3] Yet, in neither case was the shooting found to be criminal.[4] The rarity of these incidents is reflected in Florida statistics: 221,443 licenses were issued between October 1, 1987, and April 30, 1994, but only eighteen crimes involving firearms were committed by those with licenses.[5] While a statewide breakdown on the nature of those crimes is not available, Dade County records indicate that four crimes involving a permitted handgun took place there between September 1987 and August 1992 and none of those cases resulted in injury.[6]

The potential defensive nature of guns is indicated by the different rates of so-called "hot burglaries," where residents are at home when the criminals strike.[7] Almost half the burglaries in Canada and Britain, which have tough gun control laws, are "hot burglaries." By contrast, the United States, with laxer restrictions, has a "hot burglary" rate of only 13 percent. Consistent with this rate, surveys of convicted felons in America reveal that they are much more worried about armed victims than they are about running into the police. This fear of potentially armed victims causes American burglars to spend more time than their foreign counterparts "casing" a house to ensure that nobody is home. Felons frequently comment in these interviews that they avoid late-night burglaries because "that's the way to get shot."[8]

Americans defend themselves with guns between 764,000 and 3.6 million times each year, with the vast majority of cases simply involving people brandishing a gun to prevent attack.

A similar case exists for concealed handguns. The use of concealed handguns by some law-abiding citizens may create a positive externality [enjoying a benefit for which one did not pay] for others. By the very nature of these guns being concealed, criminals are unable to tell whether the victim is armed before they strike, thus raising criminals' expected costs for committing many types of crimes.

Stories of individuals using guns to defend themselves have helped motivate thirty-one states to adopt laws requiring authorities to issue, without discretion, concealed-weapons permits to qualified applicants.[9] This figure constitutes a dramatic increase from the nine states that allowed concealed weapons in 1986.[10] While many studies examine the effects of gun control,[11] and a smaller number of papers specifically address the right to carry concealed firearms,[12] these papers involve little more than either time-series or cross-sectional evidence comparing mean crime rates, and none controls for variables that normally concern economists (for example, the probability of arrest and conviction and the length of prison sentences).[13] These papers fail to recognize that it is frequently only the largest counties by population that are very restrictive when local authorities have been given discretion in granting concealed handgun permits. Therefore, state "shall issue" concealed handgun permit laws, which require permit requests be granted by the local authorities unless the individual has a criminal record or a history of significant mental illness,[14] will not alter the number of permits being issued in all counties. In other words, since rural counties generally already permit a substantial amount of concealed handguns, the effect of introducing a state law should be small in those counties.

A study on "shall issue" laws

Other papers suffer from other weaknesses. The paper by David McDowall et al.,[15] which evaluates right-to-carry provisions, was widely cited in the popular press. Yet, their study suffers from many major methodological flaws: for instance, without explanation, they pick only three cities in Florida and one city each in Mississippi and Oregon (despite the provisions involving statewide laws); and they neither use the same sample period nor the same method of picking geographical areas for each of those cities.[16]

Anecdotal evidence is widely available from both sides, with the news regularly containing stories on gun violence. While defensive uses of guns are neither as dramatic nor as frequently reported, the stories have played a large role in inducing thirty-one states to gamble that concealed handguns will deter crime by guaranteeing their citizens the right to carry concealed handguns if they do not have a criminal record or histories of significant mental illness. This constitutes a dramatic increase from the nine states that allowed concealed weapons in 1986. While the effects described by both sides exist, the question is really what the net effect of such laws is: are more lives saved or lost as a result of allowing law-abiding citizens to carry concealed handguns?

Adopting . . . "shall issue" or non-discretionary permit laws reduced murders by 8 percent, rapes by 5 percent, aggravated assaults by 7 percent, and robbery by 3 percent.

Anecdotal evidence obviously cannot resolve this debate. To provide a more systematic answer, I completed a study with David Mustard, a graduate student at the University of Chicago, analyzing the FBI's crime statistics. Our paper uses annual cross-sectional time-series county level crime data for all 3,054 U.S. counties from 1977 to 1992 to investigate the impact of "shall issue" right-to-carry firearm laws. It is also the first paper to study the questions of deterrence using these data. While many crime studies employ proxies for deterrence, such as police expenditures or general levels of imprisonment, we are able to use arrest rates by type of crime, and also, for a subset of our data, conviction rates and sentence lengths by type of crime.

We also attempt to analyze a question noted but not empirically addressed in this literature: the concern over causality between increases in handgun usage and crime rates. Is it higher crime that leads to increased handgun ownership, or the reverse? The issue is more complicated than simply whether carrying concealed firearms reduces murders because there are questions such as whether criminals might substitute between different types of crimes as well as the extent to which accidental handgun deaths might increase.

The impact of "shall issue" laws

The most conservative estimates show that adopting these so-called "shall issue" or non-discretionary permit laws reduced murders by 8 percent, rapes by 5 percent, aggravated assaults by 7 percent, and robbery by 3 percent. To put it another way, if those states that did not have concealed handgun laws in 1992 had adopted them, citizens in those states would have avoided suffering approximately 1,500 murders, 4,200 rapes, over 60,000 aggravated assaults, and 12,000 robberies. Criminals do apparently respond to deterrence.

A National Institute of Justice study estimates the costs of different types of crime based upon lost productivity, out-of-pocket expenses such as medical bills and property losses, and losses for fear, pain, suffering, and lost quality of life.[17] While there are questions about using jury awards to measure losses such as fear, pain, suffering, and lost quality of life, the estimates provide us one method of comparing the reduction in violent crimes with the increase in property crimes. The estimated gain from allowing concealed handguns is over $5.74 billion in 1992 dollars. The reduction in violent crimes represents a gain of $6.2 billion ($4.28 billion from murder, $1.4 billion from aggravated assault, $374 million from rape, and $98 million from robbery), while the increase in property crimes represents a loss of $417 million ($343 million from auto theft, $73 million from larceny, and $1.5 million from burglary).

These estimates are probably most sensitive to the value of life used.[18] Higher estimated values of life will increase the net gains from concealed handgun use, while lower values of life will reduce the gains. To the extent that people are taking greater risks towards crime because of any increased safety produced by concealed handgun laws, these numbers will underestimate the total savings from concealed handguns.

By virtue of the fact that handguns are concealed, criminals are unable to tell whether a potential victim is able to defend herself until they attack.

While the initial drop in crime is frequently small, the longer the law is in effect the larger the drop in crime will be over time. Figures 27.1 and 27.2 illustrate this relationship for murder and rape.[19] This pattern closely tracks the changes in concealed handgun permits issued over time. For example, while only 33,541 permits were issued in Florida during the first year that the law was in effect, 67,043 permits had been issued by the end of the fourth year and 192,016 permits at the end of the ninth. Where county level concealed handgun permits numbers were available (Pennsylvania and Oregon), we found direct evidence that increases in the

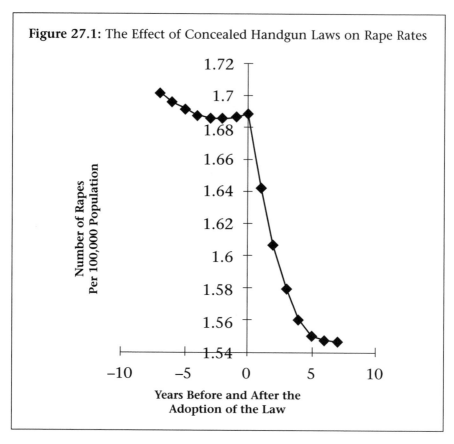

Figure 27.1: The Effect of Concealed Handgun Laws on Rape Rates

Number of Rapes Per 100,000 Population

Years Before and After the
Adoption of the Law

number of handgun permits reduced crime, though the relationships were not always statistically significant.

The benefits of concealed handguns are not limited to those who use a handgun in self-defense. By virtue of the fact that handguns are concealed, criminals are unable to tell whether a potential victim is able to defend herself until they attack, thus making it less attractive for criminals to commit crimes where they come into direct contact with victims. Citizens who have no intention of ever carrying a concealed handgun in a sense "free ride" off the crime-fighting efforts of their fellow citizens.

Yet, while some criminals avoid crimes like robbery after concealed handgun laws are passed, they do not necessarily stop committing crime entirely. Some evidence indicated that criminals substituted crimes where the risks of confronting an armed victim are much lower. Indeed, the drawback of these laws is that while violent crimes fell, property offenses like larceny (such as stealing from unattended automobiles or vending machines) and auto theft rose.

Our study also provided some surprises. While support for strict gun control laws has usually been strongest in large cities, right-to-carry laws produced the largest drops in violent crimes in counties with the highest populations and highest crime rates. For example, in counties with popu-

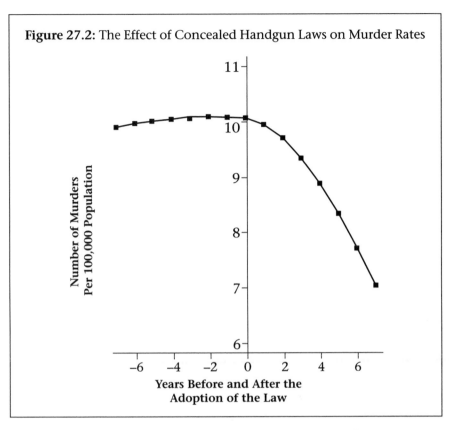

Figure 27.2: The Effect of Concealed Handgun Laws on Murder Rates

lations over 200,000, concealed handgun laws produced an average drop in murder rates of over 13 percent. The half of the counties with the highest murder rates experienced over a 10 percent drop in murders. The half of the counties with the highest rape rates saw rapes fall by over 7 percent.

The effects of concealed-carry laws

Concealed handguns also appear to be a great equalizer among the sexes. Murder rates decline when either more women or more men carry concealed handguns, but the effect is especially pronounced for women. An additional woman carrying a concealed handgun reduces the murder rate for women by about three to four times more than an additional man carrying a concealed handgun reduces the murder rate for men. Possibly, this arises because allowing a woman to defend herself with a concealed handgun represents a much larger change in her ability to defend herself than the change created by providing a man with a handgun.

Despite all the attention given to the 1994 Brady Law, which imposed waiting periods on gun purchases across the United States, our study is the first to provide direct evidence of the Brady Law's effect on crime rates. Using county level crime and punishment data available up through 1995 for Arizona, we find that the law's implementation is associated with both higher aggravated assault and rape rates. National data on state waiting period laws implies that there is no systematic relationship between either the presence or the length of the waiting period and the level of crime. However, there is some evidence that laws that punish criminals for using a gun in the commission of a crime reduce the number of crimes.

We also found some evidence on whether permitted handguns will be used in heated disputes such as at traffic accidents. With evidence now available from thirty-one states, a few of which have had these laws for many decades, there is still only one recorded incident from earlier this year in Texas, where a permitted handgun was used in a shooting following a traffic accident. Even in that one case, a grand jury found that the shooting was in self-defense, since the driver who did the shooting did so only while he was being beaten by the other driver.

And what about accidental deaths? The number of accidental handgun deaths each year is fewer than 200. Our estimates imply that if the states without "shall issue" laws were to adopt them, the increase in accidental handgun deaths would be at most nine more deaths per year. Even the largest possible increase is quite small compared to the at least 1,500 fewer murders that would be produced.

Preventing law-abiding citizens from carrying handguns does not end violence, but merely makes them more vulnerable to being attacked.

There is also the question of what effect concealed handgun laws have on determining which types of people are more likely to be murdered. Using the *Uniform Crime Reports Supplementary Homicide Reports* we were able to obtain annual state level data from 1977 to 1992 on the percent of victims by sex, race, and age, as well as information on whether the victim and the offender knew each other (whether they were members of the same family, knew each other but were not members of the same family, strangers, or the relationship was unknown).[20] Generally, the drop in murders that follows adoption of nondiscretionary concealed handgun laws is true across the entire range of potential victims. While the laws lower slightly the age of victims (consistent with the notion that concealed handguns deter crime against adults more than young people because only adults can legally carry concealed handguns), the effect is statistically insignificant. Possibly some of the benefits from adults carrying concealed handguns are conferred to younger people who may be protected by these adults.

How much confidence do we have in our results? No single study is likely to end the debate on concealed handguns, but ours provides the first systematic national evidence; and the almost 50,000 observations in our data set allow us to control for a range of factors that have never been accounted for in any previous study of crime, let alone any previous gun control study. By contrast, the largest prior study examined only 170 cities within a single year.[21] Among other variables, our regressions control for arrest and conviction rates, prison sentences, changes in handgun laws such as waiting periods or those imposing penalties when a gun is used in the commission of a crime, income, poverty, unemployment, and demographic changes.

Preventing law-abiding citizens from carrying handguns does not end violence, but merely makes them more vulnerable to being attacked. The very large size and strength of our results should at least give pause to those who oppose concealed handguns. Chances to relax regulations that potentially offer at least 8 percent drops in murder rates are difficult to ignore.

Notes

1. Gary Kleck and Marc Gertz, *Armed Resistance to Crime: The Prevalence and Nature of Self-Defense with a Gun*, 86 J. CRIM. L. & CRIMINOLOGY 150, 153, 180, 180–82 (1995). Using the National Crime Victimization Survey (NCVS), Philip J. Cook further states that each year there are "only" 80,000 to 82,000 defensive uses of guns during assaults, robberies, and household burglaries. *Id.* at 153. Unlike the surveys cited above, the NCVS is not a representative sample of the national population. Philip J. Cook, *The Technology of Personal Violence, in* 14 CRIME & JUST. 10, 11 n.4 (Michael Tonry ed., 1991). It is very easy to find people arguing that concealed handguns will have no deterrent effect. H. RICHARD UVILLER, VIRTUAL JUSTICE (1996) writes that, "[m]ore handguns lawfully in civilian hands will not reduce deaths from bullets and cannot stop the predators from enforcing their criminal demands and expressing their lethal purposes with the most effective tool they can get their hands on." *Id.* at 95.

2. Japan Economic Newswire, *U.S. Jury Clears Man Who Shot Japanese Student*, KYODO NEWS SERVICE, May 24,1993; Lori Sharn, *Violence Shoots Holes in USA's Tourist Image*, USA TODAY, Sept. 9, 1993, at 2A.

3. Dawn Lewis of Texans Against Gun Violence provided a typical reaction from gun control advocates to the grand jury decision not to charge Gordon Hale. She said, "We are appalled. This law is doing what we expected, causing senseless death." Mark Potok, *Texan Says Gun Law Saved His Life 'I Did What I Thought I Had to Do,'* USA TODAY, Mar. 22, 1996, at 3A. For a more recent evaluation of the Texas experience, see *Few Problems Reported After Allowing Concealed Handguns, Officers Say*, FORT WORTH STAR TELEGRAM, July 16,1996, at A1. By the end of June 1996, more than 82,000 permits had been issued in Texas.

4. In fact, police accidentally killed 330 innocent individuals in 1993, compared to the mere 30 innocent people accidentally killed by private citizens who mistakenly believed the victim was an intruder. John R. Lott, Jr., *Now That the Brady Law Is Law, Are You Any Safer Than Before?* PHILA. INQUIRER, Feb. 1, 1994, at A9.

5. Clayton E. Cramer and David B. Kopel, *'Shall Issue': The New Wave of Concealed Handgun Permit Laws*, 62 TENN. L. REV. 679, 691 (1995). An expanded version of this paper dated 1994 is available from the Independence Institute, Golden, Colorado. Similarly, Multnomah County, Oregon, issued 11,140 permits over the period January 1990 to October 1994 and experienced five permit holders being involved in shootings, three of which were considered justified by grand juries. Bob Barnhart, *Concealed Handgun Licensing in Multnomah County* (mimeo Intelligence/Concealed Handgun Unit: Multnomah County, October 1994). Out of the other two cases, one was fired in a domestic dispute and the other was

an accident that occurred while an assault rifle was being unloaded. *Id.*

6. Cramer and Kopel, *supra* note 5, at 691–92.

7. For example, see DAVID B. KOPEL, THE SAMURAI, THE MOUNTIE, AND THE COW-BOY 155 (1992).

8. JAMES D. WRIGHT & PETER H. ROSSI, ARMED AND CONSIDERED DANGEROUS: A SURVEY OF FELONS AND THEIR FIREARMS 145 (1986). Wright and Rossi interviewed felony prisoners in ten state correctional systems and found that 56 percent said that criminals would not attack a potential victim who was known to be armed. *Id.* They also found evidence that criminals in those states with the highest levels of civilian gun ownership worried the most about armed victims. *Id.*

    Examples of stories where people successfully defend themselves from burglaries with guns are quite common. *See, e.g., Burglar Puts 92-Year-Old in the Gun Closet and Is Shot*, N.Y. TIMES, Sept. 7,1995, at A16; George F. Will, *Are We 'A Nation of Cowards'?*, NEWSWEEK, Nov. 15, 1993 (discussing more generally the benefits produced from an armed citizenry).

9. These states are Alabama, Alaska, Arizona, Arkansas, Connecticut, Florida, Georgia, Idaho, Indiana, Kentucky, Louisiana, Maine, Mississippi, Montana, Nevada, New Hampshire, North Carolina, North Dakota, Oklahoma, Oregon, Pennsylvania, South Carolina, South Dakota, Tennessee, Texas, Utah, Vermont, Virginia, Washington, West Virginia, and Wyoming.

10. These states were Alabama, Connecticut, Indiana, Maine, New Hampshire, North Dakota, South Dakota, Vermont, and Washington. Fourteen other states provide local discretion on whether to issue permits: California, Colorado, Delaware, Hawaii, Iowa, Louisiana, Maryland, Massachusetts, Michigan, Minnesota, New Jersey, New York, Rhode Island, and South Carolina.

11. For a survey, see Gary Kleck, *Guns and Violence: An Interpretive Review of the Field*, 1 SOC. PATH. 12 (1995).

12. *See, e.g.*, Philip J. Cook et al., *Regulating Gun Markets*, 86 J. CRIM. L. & Criminology 59 (1995); Cramer and Kopel, supra note 5; David McDowall et al., *Easing Concealed Firearms Laws: Effects on Homicide in Three States*, 86 J. CRIM. L. & CRIMINOLOGY 193 (1995); Gary Kleck and E. Britt Patterson, *The Impact of Gun Control and Gun Ownership Levels on Violence Rates*, 9 J. OF QUANTITATIVE CRIMINOLOGY 249 (1993).

13. Kleck and Patterson, *supra* note 12, at 250. All 22 gun control papers studied by Kleck use either cross-sectional state or city data or use time-series data for the entire United States or a particular city.

14. Cramer and Kopel, *supra* note 5, at 680–707.

15. McDowall et al., *supra* note 12.

16. Equally damaging, the authors appear to concede in a discussion that follows their piece that their results are highly sensitive to how they define the crimes that they study. *Id.* at 202–4. Even with their strange sample selection techniques, total murders appear to fall after the passage of concealed weapon laws. Because the authors examine only murders committed with guns, there is no attempt to control for any substitution effects that may occur between different methods of murder. For an excellent discussion of the McDowall et al. paper, see Daniel D. Polsby, *Firearms*

Costs, Firearms Benefits and the Limits of Knowledge, 86 J. CRIM. L. & CRIMI-NOLOGY 207 (1995).

17. TED R. MILLER ET AL., VICTIM COSTS AND CONSEQUENCES: A NEW LOOK (1996).

18. MILLER ET AL., *supra* note 17, set the value of one life at about $3 million in 1992 dollars. *Id.* at 21.

19. *See* Figures 27.1 and 27.2. The figures were derived from the predicted values generated from regressions where separate time trends and those time trends squared were used before and after the implementation of the law. In estimating these regressions, we controlled for measures of income, unemployment, poverty, detailed demographic characteristics, changing arrest rates, population density, fixed year and county effects, as well as many other variables.

20. While county level data were provided in the *Supplementary Homicide Report*, matching these county observations with those used in the *Uniform Crime Reports* proved unusually difficult. A unique county identifier was used in the *Supplementary Homicide Report* and it was not consistent across years. In addition, some caution is suggested in using both the Mortality Detail Records and the *Supplementary Homicide Report* since the murder rates reported in both sources have relatively low correlations of less than .7 with the murder rates reported in *Uniform Crime Reports*. This is especially surprising for the *Supplementary Report* which is derived from the UCR.

21. Kleck and Patterson, *supra* note 12, at 256.

6

Concealed-Carry Laws Do Not Save Lives

Daniel Webster and Jens Ludwig

Daniel Webster is an assistant professor of health policy and management at the School of Hygiene and Public Health at Johns Hopkins University in Baltimore, Maryland. Jens Ludwig is an assistant professor of public policy at Georgetown University in the District of Columbia. In addition, Ludwig is an affiliated expert of the Johns Hopkins Center for Gun Policy and Research and a member of the National Consortium on Violence Research at Carnegie Mellon University in Pittsburgh, Pennsylvania.

Despite the claims made by John R. Lott Jr. and other pro-gun activists, laws that permit the carrying of concealed handguns do not reduce violent crimes. Criminals might in fact be more likely to shoot potential victims in order to prevent an armed response. The studies that show the positive effects of concealed-carry laws are riddled with flaws, including overemphasizing the importance of those laws when comparing crime rates in two states and confusing correlation with causation. Supporters of permissive gun laws also overestimate defensive gun use. Rather than decrease crime, the increased availability of guns will lead to more deaths.

In 1998, economist John Lott, Jr. published a book with the provocative title *More Guns, Less Crime*[1] in which he presents and interprets data to support his thesis that communities are safer when its residents are free of government restrictions on gun ownership and carrying. The book focuses primarily on two of his studies. The first, conducted with David Mustard, estimates the effects on crime attributable to state laws that allow virtually all eligible gun buyers to obtain a permit to carry a gun in public.[2] The second, conducted with William Landes, examines the effects of permissive gun carrying laws on mass shootings.[3] In each case, the authors conclude that permissive gun carrying laws result in substantial reductions in violent crime.

Another study that examines the benefits of gun ownership and carrying was conducted by Florida State University criminologists Gary Kleck and Marc Gertz,[4] and was designed to estimate the frequency with which would-be-victims of crime in the U.S. use guns to successfully defend themselves. Kleck and Gertz estimate that 2.5 million citizens use guns in self-defense each year in the U.S., a figure that exceeds the annual number of gun crimes committed (around 1 million, according to government victimization surveys).

Lott and Kleck, as well as pro-gun activists, have used these studies to argue that policies that could potentially make guns less available to citizens may cause violent crime to increase by preventing more defensive gun uses than gun crimes. This paper summarizes some of the key problems with these studies and the authors' interpretations of their findings.

The costs of permissive gun laws

Currently, 31 states have laws that require local law enforcement authorities to issue permits to carry concealed handguns to any adult applicant who does not have a felony conviction or a history of serious mental illness. Prior to the implementation of such laws, local police had discretion in issuing such permits. Because most police officers are nervous about the possibility that every traffic stop or drunk-and-disorderly might be armed, law enforcement officials in states that allow police discretion in the issuance of gun carrying permits had typically issued only a limited number of such permits.

The argument by Lott and other proponents of permissive gun-carrying laws is that if more people could legally carry guns in public spaces, the chances that criminal predators encounter well-armed would-be victims will increase. This heightened risk faced by potential attackers will in turn dissuade them from committing violent crimes in the future.

The potential costs of these laws come from the possible misuse of guns by those with concealed-carry permits, and the potential complications that such laws may pose for police efforts to prevent illegal gun carrying. Another cost from these laws comes from the possibility of an "arms race" between criminals and law-abiding citizens. Previous research suggests that this is a plausible concern. Currently, a full 75% of robbers do not use guns to commit their crimes.[5] If more potential victims start carrying handguns, those robbers who continue to perpetrate street muggings may be more likely to use guns to commit their crimes. When they do, these robbers may be more likely to shoot first and ask questions later in an attempt to preempt an armed victim response. In fact, research by Philip Cook confirms that cities where more robbers use guns to commit their crimes also have higher robbery-murder rates.[6]

Since both positive and negative effects from these laws are in principle possible, what are the net effects on the overall rate of violent crime? The results of John Lott's research (or at least his interpretation of his findings) point one way, made clear by the book's title—*More Guns, Less Crime*. But, as we will demonstrate, the evidence that permissive gun carrying laws lead to substantial reductions in crime is shaky at best.

Much of Lott's book focuses on his and David Mustard's study that was designed to estimate the effects that permissive gun carrying laws had in the first 10 states that adopted them in the U.S. To estimate the impact of these laws, Lott analyzed data on crime trends from 1977 through 1992 for 3,054 counties across the U.S. His research approach was to identify the effects of permissive gun carrying laws by comparing changes in crime rates over time in states that adopted permissive concealed-carry laws with states that did not alter their usually more restrictive laws governing the issuing of permits to carrying concealed guns. These comparisons in trends statistically control for a number of differences across counties that may affect crime; for example, he controls for differences in the age, race, and income levels of populations. Some analyses also control for the presence of laws requiring waiting periods for handgun purchases and laws requiring mandatory minimum sentences for persons convicted of committing a violent crime with a gun.

The methods used in Lott's study are relatively sophisticated and, in some ways, are an improvement on previous evaluations of gun laws. But it is very difficult to derive valid estimates of the effects of 10 state gun laws due to the need to control for other factors that influence crime trends that may also be correlated with the passage of permissive gun carrying laws. The errors made in this study, several inconsistencies in the findings, the implausible estimates that are generated, and subsequent research on the effects of permissive gun carrying laws provide convincing evidence that Lott's methods do not adequately control for these other confounding factors.

Errors in Lott's research

We will not describe in detail all of the errors contained in *More Guns, Less Crime*. Readers are referred to the work of Professor Tim Lambert of the University of New South Wales for an extensive review of these errors, and our previous explanation of errors made in the classification of certain states' gun carrying laws.

Errors aside, the fundamental problem with Lott's research can be summarized by the old social science adage "correlation is not causation." Many variables may be related to one another yet not cause one another. For example, there is a significant association between a child's shoe size and the child's writing ability. But this correlation, of course, does not prove that large shoes improve writing ability.[7]

If more potential victims start carrying handguns, those robbers who continue to perpetrate street muggings may be more likely to use guns to commit their crimes.

A similar inferential challenge lies at the heart of most policy evaluations, including Lott's study of the effects of permissive concealed-carry laws. If Florida has a lower crime rate than California, and Florida has a permissive concealed-carry law, can we conclude that the difference in crime rates is due to the gun-carrying legislation? In reality Florida and California differ along a number of dimensions, and attributing the difference in crime rates between the two states to any one factor is quite difficult. The obvious concern is that we will mistakenly attribute the difference in crime rates between Florida and California to the presence of a permissive concealed-carry law in the former, when in fact part or all of the difference will be due to other unmeasured differences across states. Lott does control for some differences between states that would explain some of the differences in crime rates. But he does not adequately control for many other factors that are almost surely relevant for a state's crime rate, including poverty, drugs (and in particular crack use and selling, which is widely thought to have been responsible for the dramatic increase in violent crime in America starting in the mid-1980's), gang activity, and police resources or strategies.

Lott tries to overcome this problem by comparing the *changes* in crime rates over time in states with versus without permissive concealed-carry laws. The idea is that unmeasured factors may cause California to have a higher crime rate than Florida, so focusing on the *change* in crime rates in Florida around the time of this state's gun-carrying law with the change observed in California around the same time will not be affected by the fact that California always has higher crime rates than Florida for reasons unrelated to the law. This research strategy assumes that the trend in crime rates in states like California and Florida would have been identical had Florida not enacted a permissive concealed-carry law.

But research by Dan Black at Syracuse University and Dan Nagin at Carnegie-Mellon show that: (1) states with permissive concealed-carry laws have violent crime trends that were different from other states even before the gun-carrying laws are enacted in that violence was increasing more in states the adopted permissive gun carrying laws than in other states in the years leading up to the permissive gun carrying law; and (2) the variables included in Lott's statistical models do a poor job of controlling for these differences in trends. As a result, differences in crime trends between states with and without permissive gun-carrying laws around the time of these laws cannot be attributed to the laws themselves, because all or part of the difference in trends around the time of the laws will be due to the unmeasured factors that caused the trends to be different before the laws went into effect. Crime trends in any particular area tend to be cyclical and regress to some long-term mean (average) after going up or down. Therefore, the reductions in violent crime observed after the introduction of permissive gun carrying laws may actually be simple regression to the mean, rather than the effects of the laws, as Lott suggests.

To his credit, Lott recognizes the potential problem with his crime-trend analysis. He attempts to remedy the problem in some of his analyses by using a more complicated statistical technique for identifying causal effects known as instrumental variables. Instrumental variables analyses are dependent on several crucial assumptions that may or may not hold in the crime data, though Lott presents none of the diagnostic tests that might help readers determine whether these assumptions are met. Instrumental variables require that the analyst identify a variable that is correlated with a state's gun carrying law, but is otherwise uncorrelated with differences across states in crime rates. One such variable that Lott uses is the proportion of a state's population that belongs to the National Rifle Association (NRA). While this variable is correlated with state concealed-carry laws, most people can recognize that NRA representation within a state is likely to be correlated with crime rates for other reasons as well, since heavy NRA states are more likely than average to be rural and to support many other "tough on crime" measures. Lott uses other instrumental variables as well, though all of them have similar problems. In fact, the statistical problems with many of his instruments were discussed in a report issued on criminal deterrence by the National Academy of Sciences in 1978.[8]

Unlike most of the other findings that Lott describes in his book, he does not translate the results from the instrumental variable analyses into estimates of the percentage reduction in violent crime associated with the adoption of permissive gun carrying laws. When Lott's findings from these analyses are translated in this manner, the estimates suggest that enacting a permissive gun carrying law will, on average, reduce homicides by 67 percent, rapes by 65 percent, and assaults by 73 percent. If true, these results suggest that if every state in the union enacted a permissive gun carrying law, our murder rate would be reduced to levels not seen in this country since 1910, roughly similar to the rate currently observed in Finland. These implausibly large estimates of the laws' effects are strong evidence that Lott's efforts to address the problem with his crime trend comparisons was unsuccessful.

Permissive laws do not reduce crime

Lott's other study of the effects of permissive gun carrying laws on multiple-victim public shootings uses the same research approach as the study discussed above, and thus suffers from the same inferential problems. This study also produces estimates of the law effects that most would consider implausibly large—an 89% reduction in multiple-victim public shootings. One indicator of the implausibility of these estimates of the effects of permissive carry laws is Gary Kleck's skepticism that permissive gun carrying laws could produce the much more modest reductions in violent crime (usually 2%–8%) that Lott more commonly trumpets. Kleck (generator of implausibly large estimates of the number of successful defensive gun uses in the U.S.) states that Lott's conclusions that permissive gun carrying laws led to substantial reductions in violent crime

> . . . could be challenged, in light of how modest the intervention was. The 1.3% of the population in places like Florida who obtained permits would represent at best only a slight increase in the share of potential crime victims who carry guns in public places. And if those who got permits were merely legitimating what they were already doing before the new laws, it would mean that there was no increase at all in carrying or in actual risks to criminals. . . . More likely, the declines in crime coinciding with relaxation of carry laws were largely attributable to other factors not controlled in the Lott and Mustard analysis.[9]

Indeed, a subsequent survey of new permit holders in North Carolina indicates that most had been taking a gun outside the home, in their vehicles, or on their person prior to obtaining the permit with little or no increased frequency in carrying after obtaining the permit.[10]

The study that Lott references to argue that permit holders are rarely arrested for crimes of violence also indicates that permit holders very rarely successfully use a gun to ward off a criminal attacker. This study examined data collected by the Dade County, Florida police during the first five years after Florida's permissive gun carrying law went into effect. During this period there were only three incidents in which a permit holder successfully used a gun in defense against a criminal attack outside the permit-holder's home.[11,12] Considering that about 100,000 violent crimes were reported to Dade County police during the five-year study period, it is hard to argue that criminals are likely to have noticed a significant change in their risk of facing a victim armed with a gun.

The evidence that permissive gun carrying laws lead to substantial reductions in crime is shaky at best.

Another way to assess whether the decreases in violent crime that Lott finds are associated with permissive gun carrying laws are actually attributable to the laws and not to unmeasured confounding factors is to see if the crime reductions are most pronounced for robberies than for other types of crimes because robberies are most likely to be committed against strangers in public places. But Lott's own research indicates that the violent crime category for which permissive gun carrying law effects were weakest (and often nonexistent) was robbery. Because even permissive gun carrying laws do not allow juveniles to legally carry guns, one should see greater reductions for victimizations of adults than of juveniles. Again, Lott's research as well as subsequent research[13] indicates that permissive gun carrying laws were not associated with greater reductions in murders of adults than of murders of juveniles.

Untruths about defensive gun use

Kleck and Gertz's claim of 2.5 million defensive gun uses per year is derived from a telephone survey of 5,000 American adults conducted in 1992. Fifty-six respondents to this survey reported that they had used a gun in self-defense during the past year. Kleck and Gertz multiply the proportion of respondents in their survey who report a defensive gun use $(X / 5,000 = Y$ percent$)$ by the number of adults in the U.S. (around 200 million) and the number of defensive gun uses equals 2.5 million per year. They estimate that in 670,000 of these incidents the would-be victims used guns when they were away from their homes.

Many people are amazed that projections about national phenomena can be made based on a telephone survey of a few thousand adults. While many surveys of this type can provide useful information about national phenomena, in this particular case the public's skepticism is warranted. The primary problem is that, even if the Kleck and Gertz's estimates were accurate, defensive gun use is a relatively rare occurrence in that only 1% of respondents reported a defensive gun use during the previous 12 months. As David Hemenway of Harvard University has pointed out, inaccurate reporting of these events by a relatively small number of respondents could lead to population projections that are orders of magnitude different from the true incidence.[14] For example, if one-half of one percent of the survey respondents incorrectly reported that they had used a gun to defend themselves against a criminal attack during the past year, the estimated number of defensive gun uses would be twice as high the true number.

Permit holders very rarely successfully use a gun to ward off a criminal attacker.

There are many reasons that respondents' reports of defensive gun use might be exaggerated. In some cases, respondents may have misjudged the level of danger they faced when they drew their gun. Survey researchers are also familiar with two types of response bias, "telescoping" and social desirability bias, that could lead to an overstated incidence of reported events such as defensive gun use. Telescoping refers to the tendency of respondents to report that salient events such as a crime victimization or a defensive gun use occurred more recently than was the case. Evidence that the Kleck-Gertz survey respondents are telescoping their recollections of their crime victimizations comes from the estimated number of robbery victimizations it produces that is nearly five times as high as the estimate derived from the National Crime Victimization Survey (NCVS). The NCVS minimizes telescoping by using shorter recall periods and a panel design that re-surveys respondents multiple times over a three-year period.

Social desirability bias refers to the tendency of respondents to over-report their actions they believe others would find admirable such as an heroic act to defend oneself or others against a criminal. There is no way to definitively determine the degree to which social desirability bias may have influenced the Kleck-Gertz estimates of defensive gun use. However, it seems likely that the nearly half of the respondents reporting defensive gun uses who indicated that they believe their defensive gun use saved their life or the life of someone else probably thought of their actions as heroic. Such incidents are regularly reported in *American Rifleman*, a monthly magazine distributed to all members of the National Rifle Association, in a manner that unequivocally portrays the incidents as heroic acts.

Given these possible sources of error, it is not surprising that surveys sometimes produce quite puzzling results. For example, in his discussion of the pitfalls of using the Kleck-Gertz survey to make population projections about the incidence of defensive gun use, David Hemenway of Harvard University cites a 1994 phone survey of 1,500 adults living in the U.S. Six percent of the respondents to this survey reported having had personal contact with aliens from another planet. This six percent could be explained, in part, by the series of questions that led up to question about contact with aliens that set up the respondent to expect that the interviewer was hoping for some alien-contact answers. In addition, some small yet non-negligible percentage of survey respondents could be expected to have mental conditions that impair their perceptions and lead them to report defensive gun incidents that did not actually happen.

Not surprisingly, the combined effects of these problems can produce population estimates that are grossly out of line with other measures of violent crime. For example, the Kleck-Gertz projection for the number of assailants wounded by armed citizens in 1992 is more than twice as high as the estimate from another study of the *total* number of people treated for gunshot wounds in a nationally representative sample of hospitals in 1994. Finally, the Kleck-Gertz survey data suggest that, in serious crimes, the victim was four times more likely than the offender to have and use a gun, a highly implausible finding given the much higher rate of gun carrying among criminals compared with other citizens.

More guns lead to more deaths

The idea that the availability of guns increased the lethality of violent crime was first established by a 1968 study of crime in Chicago by Franklin Zimring, currently a law professor at the University of California at Berkeley. Zimring showed that most homicides and other assaults stem from arguments between people, rather than premeditated gangland-style executions. In addition, he found that assaults with a firearm were much more lethal than those in which the attacker uses a knife, even though the circumstances of gun and knife attacks closely resemble each other in most respects.[15] If the number of wounds inflicted is a reflection of the attackers' homicidal intentions, assailants using knives actually demonstrated greater intent to kill their victims than did the assailants who used guns. A similar conclusion was reached when Duke University professor Philip Cook compared gun and non-gun robberies in a series of studies during the '70's and '80's.[6, 16, 17] The implication is that more guns mean more death, and policies that can keep guns from violence-prone individuals should reduce the number of homicides.

The best science indicates that more guns will lead to more deaths.

In addition to increasing the lethality of violent acts against individuals, guns enhance assailants' ability to, within seconds, wound or kill many people, including children and other innocent by-standers. It is no surprise that incidents in which assailants seriously injure or kill many people with weapons other than firearms are quite rare in the U.S. where firearms are so plentiful.

As a result, policy makers and researchers have struggled to identify ways to keep guns away from those who are most likely to misuse them, while preserving access to guns for most law-abiding adults. Among the gun control measures that are designed to reduce the availability of guns to potentially dangerous individuals include regulations that require background checks to screen eligible from ineligible buyers, registration of firearms, licensing of firearm owners, and restrictions on the number of firearms that can be legally purchased. Most of these measures have not been adequately evaluated, however, there is some evidence that background checks requirements for handgun sales have some effect in reducing violent behavior by convicted felons. Policy makers have also sought to regulate gun design with the objective of minimizing public health costs associated with gun misuse. Examples of this approach include bans on guns with fully-automatic firing mechanisms and proposals to require all new handguns to come equipped with devices that prevent unauthorized use. There is also evidence that restrictions on carrying of guns in public places, particularly in high-risk settings and often with stepped-up enforcement, can significantly reduce gun violence.[18, 19]

Although research by John Lott and Gary Kleck has challenged the prevailing view that gun regulations can reduce lethal crimes, the many limitations of Lott's and Kleck's research indicate that there is no reason to move from view of guns and violence backed by research in previous decades. Until proven otherwise, the best science indicates that more guns will lead to more deaths.

Notes

1. Lott JR Jr. *More Guns, Less Crime.* Chicago: University of Chicago Press, 1998.

2. Lott JR Jr. Mustard D. Crime, deterrence and right-to-carry concealed handguns. *Journal of Legal Studies,* 1997; 26:1–68.

3. Lott JR Jr. Landes WM. Multiple-victim public shootings, bombings, and right-to-carry concealed handgun laws. University of Chicago Law School Working Paper, 1997.

4. Kleck G, Gertz M. Armed resistance to crime: The prevalence and nature of self-defense with a gun. *Journal of Criminal Law and Criminology,* 1995 (Fall); 86:150–187.

5. Rennison CM. Criminal Victimization 1998: Changes 1997–98 with Trends 1993–98. (NCJ 176353) Bureau of Justice Statistics, U.S. Department of Justice, Washington, DC, July 1999.

6. Cook PJ. "The effect of gun availability on robbery and robbery murder: A cross-section study of fifty cities." In *Policy Studies Review Annual, Volume 3*, RH Haveman and GG Zellner (eds.). Beverly Hills, CA: Sage, 1979.

7. Kuzma JW. *Basic Statistics for the Health Sciences.* Mountain View, CA: Mayfield Publishing Company, 1984, page 159.

8. Blumstein A, Cohen J, Nagin D. Eds. *Deterrence in Incapacitation: Estimating the Effects of Criminal Sanctions on Crime Rates.* Washington, DC: National Academy Press, 1978.

9. Kleck G. *Targeting Guns: Firearms and Their Control.* New York: Aldine de Gruyter, 1997.

10. Robuck-Mangum G. "Concealed Weapon Permit Holders in North Carolina: A Descriptive Study of Handgun Carrying Behaviors." Unpublished Master's Thesis, University of North Carolina—Chapel Hill, School of Public Health, 1997.

11. There were also three incidents in which permit holders unsuccessfully attempted to use a gun in defense against a criminal attack outside the home, including one case in which a robber took the permit holder's gun away.

12. Data cited in: Cramer CE, Kopel DB. Shall issue: The new wave of concealed handgun permit laws. *Tennessee Law Review*, 1995; 62:679–758.

13. Ludwig J. Concealed-gun-carrying laws and violent crime—evidence from state panel data. *International Review of Law and Economics*, 1998; 18:239–254.

14. Hemenway D. Survey research and self-defense gun use: An explanation of extreme overestimates. *Journal of Criminal Law and Criminology*, 1998.

15. Zimring FE. Is gun control likely to reduce violent killings? *The University of Chicago Law Review*, 1968; 35:721–737.

16. Cook PJ. Reducing injury and death rates in robbery. *Policy Analysis*, 1980; 6:21–45.

17. Cook PJ. Robbery violence. *Journal of Criminal Law and Criminology*, 1987; 78:357–376.

18. Sherman LW, Shaw JW, Rogan DP. *The Kansas City gun experiment*. National Institute of Justice Research in Brief. Washington, D.C.: U.S. Dept. of Justice, Office of Justice Programs, National Institute of Justice, January 1995.

19. Fagan J, Zimring FE, Kim J. Declining homicide in New York City: A tale of two trends. *Journal of Criminal Law and Criminology*, 1998 Summer; 88(4):1277–1323.

7

Personalized Guns Can Reduce Gun Violence

Stephen P. Teret, Susan DeFrancesco,
Stephen W. Hargarten, and Krista D. Robinson

Stephen P. Teret is the director of the Johns Hopkins Center for Gun Policy and Research at the Johns Hopkins School of Public Health in Baltimore, Maryland. Susan DeFrancesco is the center's coordinator. Stephen W. Hargarten is the director of the Firearm Injury Center at the Medical College of Wisconsin in Milwaukee. Krista D. Robinson is a former project director at the center.

Personalized guns are equipped with a safety feature that allows them to be used only by their adult owners. These guns can help reduce the rates of homicide, suicide, and accidental death. Some of the technologies developed for personalized guns include magnetic encoding, touch memory, and radio frequency technology, while fingerprint-reading technology might be available in the future. Such features would make stolen guns useless to criminals and would prevent gun use by suicidal adolescents or inquisitive children. However, legislation and litigation might be necessary to encourage the firearms industry to personalize handguns.

The technology now exists to make guns that only authorized users can operate. These safer guns could cut gun-related deaths and injuries.

Children are killing children by gunfire. These deaths are occurring in homes, on the streets, and in schools. When possible solutions to this problem are discussed, conversation most often focuses on the troubled youth. Interventions involving conflict resolution programs, values teaching, reducing violence on television, and making available after-school activities and positive role models are proposed. Although each of these interventions may provide benefits, they are, even in combination, inadequate to eliminate childhood shootings. Behavior modification programs cannot possibly reach and successfully treat every troubled youth capable of creating mayhem if he or she finds an operable firearm within arm's reach.

Why personalized guns are needed

But behavior modification isn't the only possible solution. Another intervention is now being developed: the personalized gun, a weapon that will operate only for the authorized user. Personalized guns could reduce the likelihood of many gun-related injuries to children as well as adults. They could be especially effective in preventing youth suicides and unintentional shootings by young children. Personalized guns could also reduce gun violence by making the many firearms that now are stolen and later used in crime useless to criminals. Law enforcement officers, who are at risk of having their handgun taken from them and being shot by it, would be safer with a personalized gun. I 32

About 36,000 individuals died from gunshot wounds in 1995; of these, more than 5,000 were 19 years of age or younger. Suicide is among the leading causes of death for children and young adults. In 1995, more than 2,200 people between 10 and 19 years of age committed suicide in the United States, and 65 percent of these used a gun.

Adolescence is often a turbulent stage of development. Young people are prone to impulsive behavior, and studies show that thoughts of suicide occur among at least one-third of adolescents. Because firearms are among the most lethal methods of suicide, access to an operable firearm can often mean the difference between life and death for a troubled teenager. Studies have shown a strong association between the risk of adolescent suicide and home gun ownership. Although the causes of suicide are complex, personalizing guns to their adult owners should significantly reduce the risk of suicide among adolescents.

Personalized guns could . . . reduce gun violence by making the many firearms that now are stolen and later used in crime useless to criminals.

The number of unintentional deaths caused by firearms has ranged between 1,225 and 2,000 per year since 1979. Many of the victims are young children. In 1995, the most recent year for which final statistics are available, 440 people age 19 and younger, including 181 that were under 15, were unintentionally killed with guns.

Some have argued that the best way to reduce these unintentional firearm deaths is to "gun-proof" children rather than to child-proof guns. It is imprudent, however, to depend on adults' efforts to keep guns away from children and on children's efforts to avoid guns. Firearms are available in almost 40 percent of U.S. homes, and not all parents can be relied upon to store guns safely. Surveys have documented unsafe storage practices, even among those trained in gun safety.

Stolen guns contribute to the number of gun-related deaths. Experts estimate that about 500,000 guns are stolen each year. Surveys of adult and juvenile criminals indicate that thefts are a significant source of guns used in crime. Roughly one-third of the guns used by armed felons are obtained directly through theft. Many guns illegally sold to criminals on the street have been stolen from homes. Research on the guns used in crime demonstrates that many are no more than a few years old. Requiring all guns to be personalized could, therefore, limit the availability of usable guns to adult and juvenile criminals in the illegal gun market.

Ways to make guns safer

The idea of making a gun that some people cannot operate is not new. Beginning in the late 1880s, Smith & Wesson made a handgun with a grip safety and stated in its marketing materials that ". . . no ordinary child under eight can possibly discharge it." More recently, some gun manufacturers have provided trigger-locking devices with their new guns. But trigger locks require the gun owner's diligence in relocking the gun each time it has been unlocked. Also, handguns are frequently purchased because the buyer believes he or she needs and will achieve a form of immediate self-protection. These gun owners may perceive devices such as trigger locks as a hindrance when they want the gun to be immediately available. Also, some trigger locks currently on the market are so shoddy that they can easily be removed by anyone.

Today, a number of technologies are available to personalize guns. For example, magnetic encoding has long been available for the personalization of guns. Magna-Trigger™ markets a ring that contains a magnet, which, when properly aligned with a magnet installed in the grip of the gun, physically moves a lever in the grip of the firearm, allowing the gun to fire. However, the Magna-Trigger™ system is not currently built into guns as original equipment; it must be added later. Because the gun owner must take this additional step and because the magnetic force is not coded to the gun owner, this technology is not optimal.

Another technology—touch memory—was used in 1992 by Johns Hopkins University undergraduate engineering students to develop a non-firing prototype of a personalized gun. Touch memory relies on direct contact between a semiconductor chip and a reader on the grip of the gun. A code is stored on the chip, which is placed on a ring worn by the user. The gun will fire only if the reader recognizes the proper code on the chip.

Another type of personalized gun employs radio frequency technology, for which the user wears a transponder imbedded in a ring, watch, or pin attached to the user's clothing. A device within the firearm transmits low-power radio signals to the transponder, which in turn "notifies" the firearm of its presence. If the transponder code is one that has previously been entered into the firearm, the firearm "recognizes" it and is enabled. Without the receipt of that coded message, however, a movable piece within the gun remains in a position that mechanically blocks the gun from firing. One major gun manufacturer has developed prototypes of personalized handguns using radio frequency technology and expects to market these guns soon.

The personalization method of the near future appears to be fingerprint-reading technology. A gun would be programmed to recognize one or more fingerprints by means of a tiny reader. This eliminates the need for the authorized user to wear a ring or bracelet. Regardless of the technology that is ultimately chosen by most gun manufacturers, several gun magazines have advised their readers to expect personalized handguns to be readily available within the next few years.

Prices for personalized handguns will be higher than for ordinary handguns. The Magna-Trigger™ device can be fitted to some handguns at a cost of about $250, plus $40 for the ring. One gun manufacturer originally estimated that personalizing a handgun would increase the cost of the gun by about 50 percent; however, with the decreasing cost of electronics and with economies of scale, the cost of personalization should substantially decrease. Polling data show that the gun-buying public is willing to pay an increased cost for a personalized handgun.

Regulating gun safety

Most gun manufacturers have not yet indicated that they will redesign their products for safety. When the manufacturers of other products involved with injuries were slow to employ injury prevention technologies, the federal government forced them to do so. But the federal government does not mandate safety mechanisms for handguns. The Consumer Product Safety Commission, the federal agency established by Congress to oversee the safety of most consumer products, is prohibited from exercising jurisdiction over firearms. However, bills have been introduced in several states that would require new handguns to be personalized. Regulation and litigation against firearms manufacturers may also add to the pressure to personalize guns.

Important legislative and regulatory efforts have already taken place in Massachusetts. The state's attorney general promulgated the nation's first consumer protection regulations regarding handguns. The regulations require that all handguns manufactured or sold in Massachusetts be made child-resistant. If newly manufactured handguns are not personalized, then stringent warnings about the product's danger must accompany handgun sales. Bills affecting gun manufacturers' liability have also been introduced in the state legislature. The proposed legislation imposes strict liability on manufacturers and distributors of firearms for the deaths and injuries their products cause. Strict liability would not be imposed, however, if a firearm employs a mechanism or device designed to prevent anyone except the registered owner from discharging it.

When personalized guns replace present-day guns that are operable by anyone, the unauthorized use of guns by children and adolescents will decrease.

A bill introduced in California would require that concealable handguns employ a device designed to prevent use by unauthorized users or be accompanied by a warning that explains the danger of a gun that does not employ a "single-user device." A bill introduced in the Rhode Island legislature would require all handguns sold in the state to be child-resistant or personalized.

To aid legislative efforts that would require personalized guns, the Johns Hopkins Center for Gun Policy and Research has developed a model law entitled "A Model Handgun Safety Standard Act." Legislation patterned after the model law has been introduced in Pennsylvania, New York, and New Jersey.

One objection to legislation requiring handguns to be personalized is that the technology has not yet been adequately developed. But in interpreting the validity of safety legislation, courts traditionally have held that standards need not be based on existing devices. For example, in a 1983 case involving a passive-restraint standard promulgated pursuant to the National Traffic and Motor Vehicle Safety Act of 1966, the Supreme Court ruled that ". . . the Act was necessary because the industry was not sufficiently responsive to safety concerns. The Act intended that safety standards not depend on current technology and could be 'technology-forcing' in the sense of inducing the development of superior safety design."

The model handgun safety legislation mandates the development of a performance standard and provides an extended time for compliance—two features that the courts have said contribute to the determination that a standard is technologically feasible. A performance standard does not dictate the design or technology that a manufacturer must employ to comply with the law. The model law calls for adoption of a standard within 18 months of passage of the law, with compliance beginning four years after the standard is adopted.

Legislative efforts to promote the use of personalized guns can be complemented by litigation. For some time, injury prevention professionals have recognized that product liability litigation fosters injury prevention by creating a financial incentive to design safer products. One lawsuit is already being litigated in California against a gun manufacturer in a case involving a 15-year-old boy who was shot unintentionally by a friend playing with a handgun. The suit alleges that, among other theories of liability, the handgun was defective because its design did not utilize personalization technology. Additional cases against gun manufacturers for failure to personalize their products can be expected.

Firearm manufacturers need to realize the benefits of personalized guns. The threat of legislation, regulation, or litigation may be enough to convince some manufacturers to integrate available personalization technologies into their products. When personalized guns replace present-day guns that are operable by anyone, the unauthorized use of guns by children and adolescents will decrease, as will the incidence of gun-related morbidity and mortality.

8

Personalized Guns Are an Ineffective Solution to Gun Violence

Violence Policy Center

The Violence Policy Center is an educational foundation that conducts research on firearm violence, works to educate the public concerning the dangers of guns, and supports gun-control measures.

Personalized guns—guns equipped with technology that make them unusable by all but the authorized owner—will have little effect on the rate of violent crime or teen suicides. Teenagers who kill themselves with a gun often own a gun or have been given access to their parents' guns, making personalization useless. Homicides are unlikely to decrease because few people commit murder with another person's gun. While guns should be made safer, cheaper and less complicated technologies exist, including trigger locks.

What is a "smart" or "personalized" gun?

The concept behind the "smart" or "personalized" gun is to design and market a firearm which prevents anyone but an "authorized user" from firing it. Proponents of personalized guns, also called "safe" guns or "childproof" guns, argue that such technology would prevent the misuse of firearms by children and teens while rendering stolen weapons useless. The most zealous devotees of the smart gun idea present it as a virtual panacea for many categories of gun injury and death in America.

How are personalized guns supposed to work?

The very existence and feasibility of the smart gun is speculative at best. The Violence Policy Center is aware of no working, reliable model of a personalized gun such as its advocates envision. Certainly, none is actually in everyday use today.

There are as many ideas for potential personalization technology as there are people promoting the smart gun. Colt's Manufacturing Company is researching a radio transponder worn by the authorized user to activate the gun. Colt has previously announced its intention to have an early prototype of this smart gun ready for testing in the fall of 1998.

From "The False Hope of the 'Smart Gun,'" by the Violence Policy Center, www.vpc.org, 1998.

Even with this timetable, it would be years before a manufacturer could make such technology available to the general public—if they ever can. Other personalization concepts being promoted by smart gun advocates include weapons that would recognize the fingerprint or hand size of an authorized user.

One of the shortcomings of smart gun technology is that it has no impact on firearms already in circulation.

How would personalization technology apply to the guns Americans already own?

Americans now own 192 million firearms, including 65 million handguns. None, of course, are personalized. One of the shortcomings of smart gun technology is that it has no impact on firearms already in circulation. Advocates of the smart gun often make claims about its potential benefits as if all guns would be personalized as soon as any were personalized. In fact, we can expect that smart gun owners would almost always own non-personalized firearms as well. According to survey data from *Guns in America: Results of a Comprehensive National Survey on Firearms Ownership and Use*, published in 1997 by the Police Foundation, only one quarter of American adults owns a gun. Nearly three quarters of these gun owners have two or more guns, however, and over two thirds of handgun owners also own at least one rifle. In other words, most households that have guns in them would have non-personalized guns in them, unless typical gun owners disposed of all of their other firearms.

Even if gun owners did exchange all their currently owned handguns for personalized guns, they might simply be trading one lethal problem for another. The *Guns in America* survey finds that more than three quarters of handguns now possessed by private individuals hold fewer than 10 rounds of ammunition—reflecting the fact that most of these handguns are revolvers. Handguns produced today are primarily pistols with 10-round magazines. Gun owners who "trade up" to smart guns would generally get a pistol of higher caliber and capacity. Therefore, the introduction of personalized guns could greatly increase the lethality of the country's privately held gun stock.

Little effect on suicide, homicide, and accidental death

What effect would personalized guns have on suicide?

Suicide is the leading cause of firearm-related death in America (18,503 incidents in 1995). Gun owners can, of course, commit suicide using their own firearms, whether they are personalized or not. Perhaps for this reason, smart gun advocates focus particularly on teenage suicide, often using numbers suggesting that personalized guns would thwart every firearm suicide death of an American age 19 or under. This optimistic assertion fails to take into account the reality of gun use and possession by teenagers and young adults.

Many young people own guns themselves or have access to guns with parental permission. A 1998 New York Times national poll of 13- to 17-year-olds found that 15 percent owned their own gun. Obviously these teenagers are "authorized" gun users—as are many more who are granted access to their parents' guns—and personalized guns would make no difference if they attempted suicide. Older teenagers, who are most likely to have access to guns with parental approval, also account for the vast majority of teen suicides; 87 percent of suicides in the under-19 age group are committed by those between 15 and 19 years old.

What effect would personalized guns have on homicides?

It would be a fairly unusual murder that is committed by a perpetrator using someone else's gun. Homicides occur most frequently between people who know one another—often spouses, intimate acquaintances, or other family members—typically as the result of an argument. Particularly in these scenarios, there is no reason to assume that assailants would not be using their own guns, personalized or not.

What effect would personalized guns have on fatal unintentional injuries?

Smart gun advocates commonly claim the technology could stop virtually all fatalities stemming from unintentional injuries. They particularly focus on deaths of children, although they are a small portion of overall fatalities in this category. Of the 1,225 fatal cases in 1995, 181 were deaths of children under the age of 15—which could be more effectively prevented by the use of existing technology.

As for the adult deaths, a study published in the *Journal of the American Medical Association* ("Unintentional, Nonfatal Firearm-Related Injuries: A Preventable Public Health Burden," June 12, 1996) found that the most common activity associated with unintentional discharges is the cleaning of a gun, and the second most common circumstance is hunting. In both of these activities, the "authorized user" would be in control of the firearm. Obviously, personalization would make no difference in such situations.

The black market and gun industry

What effect would personalization have on the criminal black market for guns?

Many advocates claim that personalized guns would strike a serious blow to the criminal black market for guns. This promise fails to take into account the way smart gun technology would work in practice.

Manufacturers, including Colt, repeatedly emphasize that personalization technology would allow for multiple users or a series of users. This means the technology would do nothing whatsoever to stop "straw purchases" of guns-sales to a front man who then transfers the weapons on the black market to criminals or others banned from firearm possession. The straw purchaser would, of course, know the procedures necessary to "authorize" these illegal users or any other purchaser.

What effect would personalization have on the theft of firearms?

While a personalized gun may be less likely to be stolen, it is highly optimistic to assume that thieves will stop attempting to steal any of the millions of guns already owned by Americans on the off-chance they may come across a personalized gun. This is especially true since Colt promises that its personalized gun "will look like any other handgun."

Why are some in the gun industry promoting personalized guns?

The market for firearms—and especially handguns—is saturated. This presents a serious challenge to the gun industry, and some companies see personalization technology as part of the response. The advent of personalization technology would likely spur some current gun owners to purchase new smart guns—turning them into gun store customers once again. Even more significant, making smart guns available would increase the chances of selling guns to Americans who currently do not own them. A March 1997 survey conducted by the National Opinion Research Center and the Johns Hopkins Center on Gun Policy and Research found that, of respondents who were "unlikely to buy a gun in the future," 35 percent would "consider buying a handgun that would only fire for the owner of the gun." Packaged with a strong sales pitch, the technology could penetrate new markets for the gun industry, putting more families at risk from guns that they wrongly believe are "safe" or "smart."

A better approach to gun safety

Is there a better way to help prevent deaths and injuries from firearms?

Any safety device, no matter how high-tech, can address only a small percentage of the annual toll taken by firearms. Yet there are less complicated, less expensive safety mechanisms that exist today and could be integrated easily into every new gun. Adjusting the trigger pull on some handguns that currently require very little strength to fire the weapon could help prevent unintentional shootings, especially by children. Any type of "positive safety" device would also decrease the frequency of unintentional discharges. Incidents when guns are fired because people thought they were not loaded could be reduced by adding load indicators and magazine disconnects. High-quality trigger locking devices can deter suicide and unintentional injuries if they are used properly.

Firearms are currently exempt from the health and safety laws that apply to every other consumer product in America, from toasters to teddy bears. Applying those same standards to guns is the real key to reducing firearm death and injury in America. Under these standards, handguns would be banned because of their high risk and low utility. Personalization, in contrast, addresses only one aspect of a handgun's many design characteristics that make the product hazardous to users and bystanders. Incorporating new technology into guns can be a part of regulation, but not a substitute for it.

What is the view of the Violence Policy Center on personalized guns?

Personalized gun technology may prevent a very small percentage of gun-related death and injury. It could perhaps prove valuable for law enforcement officers, since a significant percentage of officers killed or wounded in the line of duty are shot with their own or their partner's service weapon.

In general, however, the smart gun falls far short of the sweeping benefits its proponents claim. Any benefits would likely be outweighed by an increase in gun-owning households. Overstating the value of personalized guns will ultimately result in public cynicism regarding policy efforts to reduce gun death and injury, and delay the implementation of truly effective solutions.

9

Lawsuits Against the Gun Industry Can Reduce Violence

Brian J. Siebel

Brian J. Siebel is a senior attorney with the Legal Action Project of the Center to Prevent Handgun Violence in Washington, D.C.

The gun industry should be sued and held liable for the harm caused by its products. Gun manufacturers have not taken advantage of technology that would keep their products out of the reach of children. The industry is also at fault because its distribution system helps funnel guns into the hands of criminals and teenagers. In addition, the gun industry has been irresponsible in its marketing of handguns and assault weapons. Lawsuits against the gun industry would be the best way to bring about reform and reduce the incidence of gun violence.

[I]n 1998,] New Orleans became the first city in the nation to file suit against the gun industry. Shortly thereafter, the city of Chicago and Cook County followed with a second lawsuit. The lawsuits struck an immediate chord with municipal and county officials across the United States, who have been facing widespread gun violence in their communities for years. Since New Orleans's filing, 31 additional cities and counties and one state have filed suit against gun manufacturers, dealers, and trade associations, with still more lawsuits under consideration.

The gun lawsuits build on the lessons learned from litigation against the tobacco industry. For decades, the tobacco industry concealed its role in creating the massive harm caused by its products, so the public tended to see tobacco-related disease as the result of a choice made by the smoker, with little relation to the industry's conduct. The wave of state and city lawsuits against tobacco companies changed that perception by uncovering the tobacco industry's wrongdoing.[1] The public now understands that the tobacco industry chose to design and market its products in certain ways—by manipulating nicotine levels, by marketing to children, by sup-

From "The Case Against the Gun Industry," by Brian J. Siebel, *Public Health Reports*, September/October 2000. Copyright © 2000 by Oxford University Press. Reprinted with permission.

pressing research findings, and by lying about product dangers—that fueled a public health crisis of huge proportions. Litigation forced tobacco companies to the bargaining table, where they finally acknowledged responsibility for the harm they had caused and agreed to pay unprecedented damages to state and city governments.

The public entity gun lawsuits are exposing gun industry misconduct in the same way. Guns cause immense harm in America. Roughly 30,000 people are killed each year with firearms, making them second only to motor vehicles as the most frequent cause of injury death in the United States.[2] In 1997, 64,000 people were treated in hospital emergency rooms for *nonfatal* firearm injuries.[3] As in the case of the tobacco industry, much of this staggering harm stems from gun industry wrongdoing in the way it designs, distributes, and markets its products. By bringing suit, cities, counties, and states can change the way the gun industry conducts itself, and thereby save lives.

Guns could be made safer

Widespread firearm misuse by unauthorized users is a serious, but preventable problem. For example, approximately one child is killed, and roughly 13 more are injured, in unintentional shootings each day.[4,5] An all-too-common scenario is a curious child or teen coming across a loaded gun in their own or a friend's home and handling it as if it were unloaded, pulling the trigger and killing or injuring another child.[6,7] The National Institute of Justice, a branch of the Justice Department, has estimated that 34% of handgun owners keep their guns loaded and unlocked.[8] Further, a 1991 General Accounting Office study found that nearly a third of unintentional firearm deaths occurred either because a very young child was able to fire the weapon or because the person firing the gun was unaware it was loaded.[9]

Another dimension of the problem is suicides with firearms among 10- to 19-year-olds, which claimed the lives of three to four young people a day in 1997.[10] From 1970 to 1990, suicide rates among 10- to 19-year-olds nearly doubled, with the higher rate attributed not to an overall increase in attempts, but to an increase in firearm-related attempts,[11,12] which are much more lethal than suicide attempts by other means.[13,14]

Roughly 30,000 people are killed each year with firearms.

The gun industry has consistently tried to ignore this mounting toll of deaths and injuries, and has falsely contended that there is nothing it can do to prevent these tragedies. Yet one way to dramatically reduce unintentional shootings and teen gun suicides is to design handguns, like automobiles, to be inaccessible to or safe from young people—by building safety devices and locks into them.[15,16] Although it is critical that parents properly secure firearms kept in the home and that all gun owners receive training and education, many injury control experts say that changing the design of a product is the most effective way to reduce injury.[15]

The use of firearm safety devices to prevent accidental shootings is not new. As early as 1884, Smith & Wesson sold a handgun that utilized a type of grip safety nicknamed a "lemon squeezer," which was designed not to be fireable by children younger than age nine.[17] Smith & Wesson sold 500,000 of the firearms before discontinuing the design in 1940. In 1912, magazine-disconnect safeties were patented to prevent shootings that commonly occur after a person has removed a pistol's ammunition magazine thinking he or she has unloaded the gun.[18] A bullet is often left hidden in the chamber, with tragic results. This simple device costs less than 50 cents to install, yet the gun industry puts them on only a few pistols. Various types of indicators alerting a user to a bullet hidden in a pistol's chamber have also been devised over the decades. The General Accounting Office and others have concluded that the use of even these simple safeties or load indicators on all firearms could save hundreds of lives each year and stop thousands of nonfatal unintentional shootings.[9]

The industry takes advantage of weaknesses in the law to market guns to criminals and juveniles.

For more than two decades, gun manufacturers have also had the ability to "personalize" guns by designing them to be self-locking, utilizing various types of key or combination devices that prevent guns from being fired when locked. One simple design uses a push-button lock in the handle of the firearm very much like the combination lock on a briefcase.[18] The device is secure when locked, but can be unlocked almost instantly by a person knowing the combination, even in the dark. Many police departments are using these products on department handguns, and the state of Maryland has passed legislation requiring this kind of internal lock for all handguns made or sold in the state by the year 2002. This kind of device can also be designed to lock itself so that, like airbags in cars, it can save a life even if the owner forgets to engage it.

Companies outside the gun industry have also begun using electronic technologies to personalize firearms. One company has incorporated fingerprint-recognition technology into handguns to truly link a firearm to the authorized user. In 1996, Colt's Manufacturing Company unveiled a prototype handgun, made by an outside vendor under a federal grant, that uses radio frequency tags to prevent the gun from firing unless the user is wearing a tag emitting a signal matching the one imbedded in the gun.[15]

Personalized gun technology could prevent even more shootings than simple safeties, including murders or assaults committed with stolen guns and most teen suicides. Roughly 500,000 guns are stolen each year in the United States, many of which are used to commit violent crimes.[19] For example, school shootings in Jonesboro, Arkansas, and Springfield, Oregon, and the 1998 murder of two police officers at the US Capitol, were committed with stolen guns wielded by unauthorized users. An informal study by the Center to Prevent Handgun Violence that looked at both intentional and unintentional shootings found that *more than half* could have been prevented if this technology had been used.[6]

Despite the life-saving value of safer gun design, only one major gun company executive—former CEO and President of Colt's Manufacturing Ron Stewart—has called on the industry to fund a research and development program to advance personalized gun technology. Unfortunately, Mr. Stewart's view has not been shared by other industry executives, including his successors at Colt's Manufacturing. Industry spokespeople continue to claim that personalized gun technology is still years away, that their current firearm designs are completely safe, and that everyone other than the industry is to blame for gun violence. Yet, a first crack in the industry's stonewalling came in October 1997, when most major handgun manufacturers agreed to voluntarily offer child safety locks for sale with new handguns, marking the first time the industry acknowledged there was something it could do to help save lives. However, the switch was motivated not to protect the safety of citizens but to stave off more restrictive legislation being considered by Congress as well as to help the industry in future litigation.[20] Under the pressure of the city, county, and state lawsuits, that initial crack has begun to expand, with some gun companies starting to make limited investments in personalized gun technologies. Even so, the industry continues to offer up dozens of new, more lethal, firearm designs each year without regard for safety.[21]

A responsible industry, when faced with overwhelming data on injuries and deaths caused by its products, would not only change product design on items yet to be sold but would *recall* and retrofit products already in consumers' hands. However, there has been no pressure from the government for the gun industry to make changes it its product designs because it was given a unique exemption from federal safety regulations at the time the Consumer Product Safety Act was passed. The city, county, and state lawsuits have the ability to apply the missing pressure.

Curbing reckless gun distribution

The lawsuits allege that the gun industry facilitates illegal gun trafficking. To sell more guns and make higher profits, the industry has established a "willfully blind" distribution system, which ultimately funnels hundreds of thousands of guns from the legal marketplace into criminals' and juveniles' hands.

Firearms are distributed through a *primary* market, consisting of all transactions involving the licensed gun industry, and a *secondary* market, in which both buyers and sellers are unlicensed.[22,23] In the primary market, the three layers of sellers—manufacturers, distributors, and dealers—are all federally licensed and must comply with certain limited paperwork requirements, including record keeping and background checks. Once an individual buys a firearm, however, there is little or no federal regulation placed on reselling that weapon in the secondary market.

Gun manufacturers know that the system can be readily subverted by firearms dealers willing to look the other way when people with clean criminal records buy guns on behalf of others who are disqualified. Law enforcement's ability to curb these illegal sales is constrained by limits on the number of federal investigators overseeing the industry's sales in the primary market; congressional restrictions on computerizing records; and broad legal loopholes that make trafficking convictions difficult to secure. These constraints are the result of heavy lobbying by the gun industry and the National Rifle Association.

According to the US Bureau of Alcohol, Tobacco and Firearms (ATF), "[v]irtually all new firearms used in crime first pass through the legitimate distribution system of federally licensed firearms dealers,"[24] and a substantial portion of handguns sold through this legal marketplace ends up being used in crime.[24-26]

Sales to "straw purchasers [people who buy guns for those who would not pass background checks]" are a leading source of firearm diversions. Indeed, one major federal study of gun trafficking found that straw purchasing accounted for almost 50% of the firearms trafficked into crime.[27] Multiple sale schemes involving hundreds, or even thousands, of straw-purchased guns have also been well documented.[24,25] Evidence suggests that, among guns found at crime scenes, straw-purchased guns are twice as likely as other guns to be found in a state other than where they were bought, indicating their important role in interstate trafficking.[28]

Gun manufacturers have . . . acted irresponsibly in marketing guns as a way to increase the safety of gun owners and their families.

Corrupt firearms dealers are also a significant part of the problem. Undercover sting operations in Chicago, Detroit, and Gary, Indiana, have proved that dealers are loath to turn away paying customers, even if they openly admit to being criminals or juveniles. Chicago launched an extensive undercover investigation in 1998. Over a three-month period, the Chicago Police Department sent two-person teams into the 12 gun stores ringing the city that had sold the highest numbers of guns traced to crimes within the city. Both agents carried identification indicating that they lived in Chicago, where it has been illegal to own handguns since 1982. Only one of the agents carried a firearm owner identification card, which is required under Illinois law to purchase a firearm in the state. The agent who did *not* have the required card nevertheless did the talking, placed the cash on the counter, and walked out with the gun. The agents also openly bragged about needing the gun to "settle a score," to resell to drug gangs, or to use in other criminal enterprises, yet in each case the suburban dealer sold the firearm. Some dealers even counseled the agents in how to avoid federal paperwork that might trigger an investigation. The dealers approached in Michigan and Indiana engaged in similar misconduct even after the Chicago sting was aired nationally on *60 Minutes*. One Michigan dealer was captured on videotape saying, "It's highly illegal," yet went ahead and made the sale. Some dealers have pumped literally thousands of guns into the illegal market.[29,30]

The industry takes advantage of weaknesses in the law to market guns to criminals and juveniles. For example, evidence presented in a case in New York suggests that the industry deliberately targets areas with tax gun control laws, knowing that guns purchased there will be trafficked into states and cities with tougher gun laws.[31] A sworn affidavit issued by a former Senior Vice-President of Marketing and Sales at Smith & Wesson in this case admitted the industry's complicity:

> The company and the industry as a whole are fully aware of the extent of the criminal misuse of firearms. The company and the industry are also aware that the black market in firearms is not simply the result of stolen guns but is due to the seepage of guns into the illicit market from multiple thousands of unsupervised federal firearms licensees. In spite of their knowledge, however, the industry's position has consistently been to take no independent action to ensure responsible distribution practices.[32]

If the gun industry exercised control over its distribution network, firearms trafficking could be dramatically reduced. A system of training, monitoring, and disciplining dealers could be instituted, much in the way that certain businesses require dealers to be "authorized" before being able to sell the manufacturer's product line. Other industries selling products for which the danger of misuse is high have instituted marketing controls, including franchising retail sales outlets, restricting retail sales through distribution contracts, and requiring safe sales practices at the retail level.[33]

Smith & Wesson takes action

This point was recently underscored by leading gun maker Smith & Wesson, which [in 1999] started requiring gun dealers stocking its products to sign a new "Code of Responsible Business Practices" or be cut off. Unfortunately, the Code is very weak, merely requiring dealers to maintain store premises, to not "knowingly" sell firearms to straw purchasers or otherwise violate the law, and to comply with other minimal provisions. Smith & Wesson has the right under the Code to terminate dealers who have been sued by municipalities for negligent distribution practices.

Subsequent to issuing this weak Code, Smith & Wesson reached an historic settlement agreement in March 2000 with the Department of Housing and Urban Development, two state Attorneys General, and a number of the cities that had sued the company, which required Smith & Wesson to initiate more dramatic changes in the way it marketed guns. The agreement requires the gun maker to sell guns only through "authorized" distributors and dealers, who in turn must sign on to stringent terms to become authorized, including independent monitoring of their ongoing compliance with the agreement. The agreement also commits Smith & Wesson to making significant improvements in gun safety.

By signing this agreement, Smith & Wesson stands alone in acknowledging that the gun industry could take steps to prevent the diversion of guns to the criminal marketplace. The rest of the industry pretends that it does not know, and cannot control, where its guns end up. The gun industry apparently takes this "see no evil" approach regarding the funneling of guns to crime because it reaps huge profits on guns channeled to criminals through its legal but lax distribution system. Moreover, by selling guns through middlemen distributors and dealers over whom the industry scrupulously avoids control, manufacturers seek to insulate themselves from liability.

The city, county, and state lawsuits attack this misconduct head-on by complaining that the industry's willfully blind distribution system has created public nuisances in these communities, and several courts have allowed these cases to proceed toward trial. The suits build on a legal victory secured in 1999 in which a Brooklyn jury concluded that 15 major gun manufacturers negligently distributed firearms.[34] The court upheld the jury verdict, finding that gun manufacturers had a duty to distribute firearms responsibly and could control their distribution network. Their failure to do so caused firearms to fall into the wrong hands, where they would foreseeably be used in crime.

Challenging deceptive advertising

Gun manufacturers have also acted irresponsibly in marketing guns as a way to increase the safety of gun owners and their families, when empirical research has demonstrated that just the opposite is true.[35-37] One major case study shows that a gun in the home is four times as likely to be involved in a fatal or nonfatal unintentional shooting as it is to be used to injure or kill in self-defense, seven times as likely to be involved in a criminal assault or homicide, and 11 times as likely to be involved in a suicide attempt.[37] Despite these findings, the gun industry has circulated numerous advertisements, often depicting mothers and young children, urging homeowners to purchase handguns for home protection.[38,39]

In 1996, the Center to Prevent Handgun Violence, joined by numerous public health organizations and 75 noted public health researchers, filed a petition with the Federal Trade Commission challenging the industry's advertising as unfair and deceptive.[40] Numerous cities and counties have also attacked this problem in their lawsuits, alleging that the industry's misconduct has caused preventable local shootings to which the city or county must respond.

> *Forcing the industry to incorporate feasible safety devices in all guns . . . could prevent thousands of injuries and deaths, most importantly among children.*

Litigation has already demonstrated that the gun industry markets high-firepower assault weapons that have no legitimate sporting or self-defense use but are perfectly suited for criminals. The Center's Legal Action Project, with which the present author is affiliated, has brought lawsuits against gun manufacturers for negligent marketing of these weapons of mass destruction. One of the most significant of these cases, *Merrill v. Navegar*,[41] led to the first appellate decision in the US holding that a gun manufacturer could be liable for negligence leading to violence. That decision is now on appeal in the California Supreme Court. The *Merrill* lawsuit stemmed from a July 1993 rampage by a man armed with two TEC-9 assault pistols and hundreds of rounds of ammunition that enabled him to kill eight people and injure six others in a San Francisco office building in a matter of minutes. The lawsuit alleged that because Navegar designed the TEC-9 for mass destruction, it was negligent to sell this assault pistol to the general public, as it was foreseeable that the guns would enable a criminal to carry out such a mass assault. Considerable evidence obtained through discovery helped prove this allegation, and showed how consciously the company had targeted the criminal market, including advertising its gun as having "an excellent resistance to fingerprints."[41]

A call for reform

Although firearm injuries and deaths obviously impact the victims and their families the hardest, gun violence also creates significant problems and costs for public authorities responsible for protecting public welfare and keeping society safe. Cities, counties, and states have been stuck with billions of dollars in costs directly resulting from gun violence. These costs include outlays for injuries to public property, medical care, police investigations, emergency rescue services, coroner services, jails and prisons, security at schools and other public buildings, funeral services for unknown victims, disability benefits, and youth intervention programs. In addition, there are numerous indirect costs, including lost tax revenues from declining real estate values in neighborhoods beset by gun violence.

Several recent studies have attempted to estimate the total public costs associated with firearm-related injuries. The studies have arrived at the same conclusion: the costs are exceptionally high for the taxpaying public.[42,43] For example, the *Los Angeles Times* did a report on the public costs stemming from the experience of one teenager, now a paraplegic as a result of a gunshot wound, estimating a total public cost of more than a million dollars for a single shooting victim.[44] Given that gun violence disproportionately affects the poor and that gunshot victims typically do not have health insurance,[45,46] firearm injuries clearly place an enormous financial burden on the public each year.

By pressing for recovery of at least some of these costs, lawsuits against the gun industry can bring about reforms, as the settlement agreement with Smith & Wesson has shown. Forcing the industry to incorporate feasible safety devices in all guns—especially locking technology to prevent unauthorized access and misuse—could prevent thousands of injuries and deaths, most importantly among children. Similar effects would likely flow once the gun industry stops duping the public into believing that guns increase home security, when empirical data prove that the opposite is true. Finally, the greatest benefits may come from making the industry tighten controls over its lax distribution network, thereby choking off the major gun pipeline for criminals, juveniles, and other inappropriate gun users. These are laudable goals, and the cities and counties that have filed suit to bring about these reforms deserve to be commended.

Notes

1. Kelder GE Jr, Daynard RA, The role of litigation in the effective control of the sale and use of tobacco. Stanford Law and Policy Rev 1997;8:63–98.
2. Murphy L. Deaths: final data for 1998. Natl Vital Stat Rep 2000;48(11): 1–105.
3. Nonfatal and fatal firearm-related injuries—United States, 1993–1997.

MMWR Morb Mortal Wkly Rep 1999;48:1029–34.

4. CDC Wonder. National Center for Health Statistics, unpublished data from the Vital Statistics System: year 1998: age range 0–19 years; injury codes 922.0–922.9 [cited 2000 Dec 4]. Available from: URL: http://wonder. cdc.gov/mortsql.shtml.

5. Sinauer N, Annest JL, Mercy JA. Unintentional, nonfatal firearm-related injuries: a preventable public health burden, JAMA 1996:275:1740–3.

6. Center to Prevent Handgun Violence. A school year in the U.S.A. Washington: Center to Prevent Handgun Violence; 1998 Oct.

7. Violence Policy Center. Kids shooting kids. Washington: Violence Policy Center; 1997 Mar.

8. Police Foundation. Guns in America: results of a comprehensive national survey on firearms ownership and use. Washington: Police Foundation; 1997.

9. General Accounting Office (US). Accidental shootings: many deaths and injuries caused by firearms could be prevented. Washington: GAO; 1991 Mar. Pub. No.: GAO/PEMD-91-9.

10. CDC Wonder. National Center for Health Statistics, unpublished data from the Vital Statistics System: year 1997: age range 10–19 years; injury codes 955.0–955.4 [cited 2000 Dec 4]. Available from: URL: http://wonder. cdc.gov/mortsql.shtml.

11. From the Centers for Disease Control and Prevention. Suicide among children, adolescents, and young adults—United States, 1980–1992. JAMA 1995:274:451–2.

12. Kachur SP, Potter LB, James SP, Powell KE. Suicide in the United States, 1980–1992. Atlanta: Centers for Disease Control and Prevention (US); 1995.

13. Katcher ML. Firearm injuries among children and adolescents. 1: the facts. Wis Med J 1994;93:511–15.

14. Fatal and nonfatal suicide attempts among adolescents—Oregon, 1988–1993, MMWR Morb Mortal Wkly Rep 1995;44:312–15,321–3.

15. Polston MD, Weil DS. Unsafe by design: using tort actions to reduce firearm-related injuries. Stanford Law and Policy Rev 1997;8:13–24.

16. Hemenway D, Weil D. Phasers on stun: the case for less lethal weapons. J Policy Analysis & Management 1990;9:94–8.

17. Robinson KD, Teret SP, Vernick JS, Webster DW. Personalized guns: reducing gun deaths through design changes. Baltimore: Johns Hopkins Center for Gun Policy and Research; 1996.

18. Berg SO. Magazine safeties: important safety design. AFTE J 1993; Oct.

19. Cook PJ, Molliconi D, Cole TB. Regulating gun markets. J Criminal Law & Criminology 1995;86:59–92.

20. Wayne L. Gun makers learn from tobacco fight. NY Times 1997 Dec 18.

21. Diaz T. Making a killing: the business of guns in America. New York: New Press; 1999.

22. Polston MD. Civil liability for high risk gun sales: an approach to combat gun trafficking. Seton Hall Legislative J 1995;19:821–55.

23. Wachtel J. Sources of crime guns in Los Angeles, California. Policing: An International Journal of Police Strategies and Management 1998;21:220–39.

24. Department of the Treasury (US). A progress report: gun dealer licensing & illegal gun trafficking (statement of Raymond W. Kelly, Under Secretary). Washington: Department of Treasury; 1997 Jan.

25. Department of the Treasury (US), Bureau of Alcohol, Tobacco and Firearms. The Youth Crime Gun Interdiction Initiative: the illegal youth firearms markets in 17 communities. Washington: Department of Treasury; 1997 Jul.

26. Department of the Treasury (US), Department of Justice (US). 27 cities report: gun crimes in the age group 18–20. Washington: Departments of Treasury and Justice; 1999 June 4.

27. ATF Performance Report: the Youth Crime Gun Interdiction Initiative. Washington: Department of Treasury; 1999 Feb.

28. Testimony of Sarah Brady, Chair, Handgun Control, Inc., before Senate Judiciary Committee (Sept. 2, 1998). Washington: Handgun Control, Inc.; 1998.

29. Department of the Treasury (US), Bureau of Alcohol, Tobacco and Firearms. Following the gun: enforcing federal laws against firearms traffickers. Washington: Department of Treasury; 2000 Jun.

30. Department of the Treasury (US), Bureau of Alcohol, Tobacco and Firearms. Commerce in firearms in the United States. Washington: Department of the Treasury; 2000 Feb.

31. Expert Report of Lucy Allen and Jonathan Portes (May 1, 1998) (filed in Hamilton v. Accu-Tek, 62 F, Supp. 2d 802 (E.D.N.Y. 1999)).

32. Affidavit of Robert I. Hass 20–21 (Feb. 20, 1996) (filed in Hamilton v. Accu-Tek, 62 F, Supp. 2d 802 (E.D.N.Y. 1999)).

33. Expert Report of David Stewart (May 1, 1998) (filed in Hamilton v. Accu-Tek, 62 F, Supp. 2d 802 (E.D.N.Y. 1999)).

34. Hamilton v. Accu-Tek, 62 F, Supp. 2d 802 (E.D.N.Y. 1999).

35. Kellermann AL, Somes G, Rivara FP, Lee RL, Banton JG. Injuries and deaths due to firearms in the home. J Trauma: Injury Infect Crit Care 1998;45:263–7.

36. Bailey JE, Kellermann AL, Somes GW, Banton JG, Rivara FP, Rushforth NP. Risk factors for violent death of women in the home. Arch Intern Med 1997;157:777–82.

37. Cummings P, Koepsell TD, Grossman DC, Savarino J, Thompson RS. The association between the purchase of a handgun and homicide or suicide. Am J Public Health 1997;87:974–8.

38. Hanson JD, Kysar DA. Taking behavioralism seriously: some evidence of market manipulation. Harvard Law Rev 1999;112:1420–67.

39. David Kairys, Legal claims of cities against the manufacturers of handguns. Temple Law Rev 1998;71:1–21.

40. Litigating for gun industry reform. Petition before the Federal Trade Commission of the Center to Prevent Handgun Violence; American Academy of Pediatrics; American Public Health Association; American As-

sociation of Suicidology; American Academy of Child and Adolescent Psychiatry; and National Association of Children's Hospitals and Related Institutions, Feb. 14, 1996 [cited 2000 Dec 4]. Available from: URL: http://www.gunlawsuits. com/litigating/articles/ftcfiling.asp

41. Merrill v. Navegar, 75 Cal. App. 4th 500, 562 (1999), review granted, 991 P.2d 755 (2000).

42. Cook P, Ludwig J. Gun violence: the real costs. New York: Oxford University Press; 2000.

43. Miller TR, Cohen MA. Costs of gunshot and cut/stab wounds in the United States, with some Canadian comparisons. Accid Anal Prev 1997;29:329–41.

44. Sipchen B. Putting a price tag on violence. Los Angeles Times 1994 Jun 5; Sect. A:22.

45. Gunderson L. The financial costs of gun violence. Ann Intern Med 1999;131:483–4.

46. Vasser MJ, Kizer KW. Hospitalizations for firearm-related injuries: a population-based study of 9562 patients. JAMA 1996:275:1734–9.

10

Lawsuits Against the Gun Industry Violate the Second Amendment

Bob Barr

Bob Barr is a Republican congressman from Georgia who serves on the House Judiciary Committee.

One approach used by antigun activists to reduce violence is filing lawsuits against gun manufacturers, based on the argument that these companies should be held responsible when their products are used illegally. Such lawsuits violate the Second Amendment because they disregard the fact that the right to bear arms "shall not be infringed." Many publications supporting gun control have agreed that lawsuits against the gun industry are unreasonable and erode the notion of personal accountability. If antigun activists want to ban gun ownership, they should work to repeal the Second Amendment rather than abuse the judicial system.

Visualize this: Conspiring around a conference table on the top floor of a large downtown glass-and-steel office building are the top representatives from the major American social conservative and feminist organizations. The office belongs to a major law firm, and the meeting has been called to draft a groundbreaking new lawsuit.

The people seated at the table are, to say the least, unlikely allies. However, they are united by a common desire to rid America of books and magazines some sociological studies have indicated contribute to violence against women, as well as disintegration of the family unit.

The group begins to carefully craft a lawsuit at the eager prodding of dozens of contingency-fee lawyers with visions of multimillion-dollar fees dancing in their heads. The lawsuit will be filed on behalf of cities that treat crime victims and spend millions keeping divorce courts open. It will target publishers, of course, as well as bookstores—from Barnes and Noble to neighborhood independents—who distribute such products. Its goal is to force the publishing industry either to stop distributing certain products or to accept a costly legal settlement.

Predicting the popular reaction to such lawsuits is quite easy: The American Civil Liberties Union, or ACLU, and other groups would go ballistic. The editorial pages of every major newspaper and the anchors of every news network roundly would decry such an assault on the First Amendment. Protests would be staged, boycotts would be called and tort-reform legislation would gain new life in Congress.

Ridiculous lawsuits

Compare the reaction to this fictional scenario with one that is occurring today, in real life. A band of seasoned anti-gun activists have joined hands with big-city mayors and trial lawyers to sue the firearms industry. Their goal is simple: to use the courts to effectively repeal the Second Amendment to the Constitution. After failing to take away our right to keep and bear arms in Congress and state legislatures, they aim to do it via the judicial process, by bankrupting manufacturers who make firearms and stores that sell them.

Where is the substantive difference between the hypothetical situation mentioned above and the actual lawsuits being filed against gun manufacturers? Such lawsuits are based on the ridiculous theory that the manufacturer of a legal product, subject to more than 20,000 federal, state and local regulations, should be held responsible when that product is used illegally by a criminal.

In a word, none. There's no difference.

Both lawsuits attack industries explicitly protected by the Bill of Rights: bookstores by the First Amendment and gun manufacturers by the Second Amendment. Both lawsuits are based on the shopworn theory of ambulance-chasing trial lawyers everywhere: File as many lawsuits as you can, use them to coerce settlements and, if that fails, keep filing them until you eventually succeed in picking a jury willing to buy whatever legal theory you're selling. In other words, keep rolling the dice in the hope you'll eventually hit the jackpot. As a bonus, with each roll the legitimate industry on which you're preying is forced to foot costly legal bills and endure negative publicity, increasing your chances of wearing them down and extorting a settlement.

If the two situations are so similar, where is the outrage at the campaign mounted against firearms manufacturers? Where are the amicus curiae briefs by the ACLU? Where are the floor speeches by members of Congress? Why do liberals who would venture into the waters of civil disobedience to protect the First Amendment endorse or ignore a blatant attempt to deprive Americans of their Second Amendment rights?

The confusion of many civil libertarians on this issue stems from a unique skill they have developed over time. They're like certain species of trout that lose their sight after successive generations of dwelling in the total darkness of caves. They have acquired a peculiar ability to read the entire Constitution without ever seeing the following words: "The right of the people to keep and bear arms, shall not be infringed."

To be sure, not everyone has been silent. The *Boston Globe* (a supporter of gun control), wrote on March 1, 1999 that, "[m]aking manufacturers liable for the actions of others, however, stretches the boundaries beyond all reasonable limits in a cause that needs all of the sensible strategy it can get."

The New Republic, a flagship journal of the left, also has blasted the lawsuits. On the same day as the *Globe* editorial, it wrote:

"In their suits against gun manufacturers, the cities would take the erosion [of personal responsibility] to a dangerous new level, further weakening the already battered notion of individual accountability upon which our democratic culture depends. . . . Is the next step a class-action suit seeking huge money damages from car manufacturers because of the costs of drunken-driving deaths and joyriding by underage car thieves?"

Clearly, there is a disconnect between thinking liberals and greedy liberals on this issue. Principled thinkers on both sides of the aisle realize standing by idly while a constitutionally protected industry is systematically bankrupted is neither a productive nor a principled way to protect freedom. As numerous commentators have pointed out, if firearms manufacturers fall prey to these tactics, the precedent will be used again and again. Whether it is suing Anheuser-Busch on behalf of victims of drunk drivers or the Ford Motor Co. on the same theory, other industries soon would find themselves in the trial lawyers' crosshairs.

The true motivation

However, you do have to give the mayors who are filing these lawsuits some credit. They've been very careful to talk in terms that carefully camouflage the true motivation of their lawsuits. To get an idea of the real motivation, one need look no further than Atlanta in my home state.

First, a few facts. According to a recent story in the *Atlanta Journal-Constitution*, the Atlanta Police Department has a 19 percent vacancy rate. Applications to the department dropped 15 percent in 1998. Furthermore, a survey [in 1998] found that an image of crime-ridden streets is one of the biggest factors driving conventions away from the city. Even worse, a Georgia Bureau of Investigation audit found that the department has been underreporting crimes to keep its crime statistics lower than they really are. For example, the department failed to report 498 robberies, 108 motor-vehicle thefts and 56 rapes. Needless to say, one would have a difficult time arguing Atlanta as a model of effective law enforcement.

No matter how absurd the claims behind these lawsuits, there are a handful of juries willing to hand out awards based on them.

Fiscally, the city's situation is not much better. According to news reports, the city's chief financial officer recently sent a memo to all departments asking them to identify 18 percent cuts in their budgets to make up for a large budget deficit, predicted by some experts to exceed $50 million.

Where does this leave Atlanta Mayor Bill Campbell? He desperately needs two things: The first is a bogeyman to blame for Atlanta's crime, thereby getting Atlanta's much-maligned police department off the hook. The second is a financial windfall so he can avoid doing things such as reducing the approximately $1 million the city annually spends on a small army of publicists—36 at last count—to sing the mayor's praises.

What better solution to these problems than suing gun manufacturers? Blaming inanimate objects for the actions of criminals provides a welcome alternative to a city that appears to be having significant trouble effectively fighting crime. The deal only is sweetened by the possibility of winning a multimillion-dollar judgment. In the process, a cherished constitutional right will be damaged, jobs will be lost and consumers will be forced to pay higher prices to purchase lawful products.

These lawsuits do raise some interesting questions. If, for example, these mayors believe firearms are defective, have they warned their police officers of this disturbing fact? Or, if trigger locks, load indicators and smart guns are such great ideas, why haven't they equipped their departments with them and mandated that every gun owned by every officer in their homes or cars be outfitted with such safety devices?

A remedy to lawsuits

Even some who oppose these lawsuits argue that allowing them to be settled solely via the judicial process is the right solution. Unfortunately, such a course has several drawbacks. First, it does nothing to remedy the short-term effects of legal harassment. The trial lawyers behind these lawsuits have tremendous financial resources. It is quite likely they will be able to use those resources to bankrupt smaller gun manufacturers before the cases are even fully litigated. It also does not take into account that no matter how absurd the claims behind these lawsuits, there are a handful of juries willing to hand out awards based on them and other bogus but sympathy-inducing theories. Finally, leaving this issue up to the courts will not prevent the widespread economic damage that is sure to ensue if the premise of these lawsuits is extended to other industries.

Clearly, a legislative remedy for these lawsuits is needed. Over the years, Congress has crafted similar legislation to address predatory lawsuits against others, such as manufacturers of small aircraft and volunteers for charitable organizations. In this Congress, I have introduced HR1032, the bipartisan Firearms Heritage Protection Act, which will ban lawsuits against firearms manufacturers or dealers based on the unlawful use of their products.

Our legislation does not prevent anyone from suing a gun manufacturer if they are injured by a defective firearm, nor does it stop anyone from suing a firearms dealer when they knowingly sell a gun to a criminal, which always has been the legal standard in America. It simply aims to restore reason, accountability and sanity to a legal system that is being taken for a ride by trial lawyers. This legislation simply maintains the status quo to protect a lawful industry from being singled out for special punishment.

Those who support gun control should argue their case in the halls of Congress and the state legislatures. Those who would ban the private ownership of firearms should work to repeal the Second Amendment. However, it would be unacceptable to abuse the judicial system to restrict the First Amendment, and it is just as unacceptable to use the same tactic to work toward judicial repeal of the Second Amendment.

11

The Brady Law Has Led to a Drop in Violent Crime

Brady Center to Prevent Gun Violence

The Brady Center to Prevent Gun Violence seeks to reduce gun violence through education, research, legal advocacy, and outreach to the entertainment community.

The Brady Law—which instituted a background check and waiting period prior to commercial gun purchases—has helped decrease crime and save lives. The law has reduced the availability of guns and their subsequent use by criminals in all states, including those that already required background checks. Since the implementation of the act in 1994, gun use by violent criminals in fatal robberies and assaults has declined. In order to further reduce gun violence, gun registration and background checks on private sales must be implemented.

I n August 2000, the *Journal of the American Medical Association* [published] "Homicide and Suicide Rates Associated with Implementation of the Brady Handgun Violence Prevention Act" by Dr. Jens Ludwig of Georgetown University and Dr. Phil Cook of Duke University. . . . We expect the gun lobby to cite this study as "proof" that gun laws don't work, as an argument against proposals like closing the gun show loophole, and as a rallying cry to roll back commonsense measures such as the Brady Law, the Assault Weapons Ban and any number of other federal, state and local gun laws. However, even a cursory reading of the Ludwig/Cook study shows that our nation's gun laws need to be strengthened, not weakened—quite the opposite conclusion that the gun lobby will impute to it.

The following Q&A offers an analysis of the Ludwig/Cook study and places it in context with other studies that examine the effectiveness of the Brady Law:

Q: Does the Ludwig/Cook paper show that the Brady Law had no impact on homicides?

A: No. The only conclusion that can be drawn from the Ludwig/Cook paper is that, after the Brady Law was passed, homicide did not decline faster in the states that had just adopted the Brady Law compared to the states that already had tighter gun laws. This is because the effect of Brady was national, not just confined to Brady states.

The authors wrote:

> In particular, we find no differences in homicides or firearm homicides to adult victims in the 32 treatment states directly subject to the Brady provisions compared with the remaining control states.

The Brady Law affects all states

The reason Brady would have an impact on homicide in all states is because, previous to Brady, states with tight gun laws were being flooded with crime guns purchased in states without a background check or waiting period. As other research described below shows, the Brady Law actually reduced the availability of crime guns and criminal gun use in both Brady and non-Brady states. States that implemented the law are "Brady states." States that already had a background check are "non-Brady states."

For example, New York State already had a background check before the Brady Law was passed and criminals were heavily dependent on guns from states like Ohio, Georgia, Mississippi, and Alabama—states that did not have a background check system until required to do so by Brady. After implementation of the Brady Law, we might instinctively expect that the crime rate in Ohio and Georgia would decline faster than in New York because the law made it more difficult for criminals to buy guns in states that had not previously required background checks. However, because Brady disrupted interstate gun trafficking, New York and other non-Brady states also experienced a drop in crime. Why? Because Ohio, Georgia and the other Brady states supplied many of the guns used by criminals in non-Brady states—guns that became much more difficult to acquire after Brady took effect.

Understanding that Brady has had an impact on gun availability and criminal gun use in all states and not just those states that were required to implement the law is key to understanding the results of the Ludwig/Cook paper. In fact, the authors acknowledge that they would not be able to detect a reduction in homicide if the law had a similar impact on homicides in both the Brady and non-Brady states:

> If implementation of the Brady Act was associated with a reduction in homicide rates of similar magnitude in control [non-Brady] states as in treatment [Brady] states, our comparisons of treatment and control state trends would have failed to detect it.

Q: So, is there any evidence that the Brady Law had an impact on gun availability and/or on the criminal use of guns in non-Brady states?

A: Yes, but that evidence was not developed in the Ludwig/Cook paper.

The Bureau of Alcohol, Tobacco and Firearms (ATF) has documented the importance of interstate gun trafficking as a source of crime guns (*Following the Gun: Enforcing Federal Laws Against Firearms Traffickers*. June

2000). For example, in the *Youth Crime Gun Interdiction Initiative Trace Analysis Reports: 27 Communities* (February 1999), the ATF showed that, of the crime guns recovered in New York City that could be traced, only 15.6% were originally purchased from gun dealers in New York State. The vast majority of traceable crime guns came from outside New York, and at least 34.7% of the crime guns traced came from states subject to the Brady Law (GA, 8.8%; NC, 8.3%; SC, 7.0%; OH, 4.2%; AL, 3.3%; and TX, 3.1%). New York was exempt from Brady because it had its own background check system in place when the law was enacted, making criminals dependent on guns purchased in states that weren't conducting background checks. Implementation of Brady in those states reduced the available supply of crime guns in New York and other non-Brady states. This impact of Brady was proven by the analysis presented in *Traffic Stop*, a September 1997 study released by the Center to Prevent Handgun Violence.

The Brady Law had a disruptive impact on interstate gun trafficking from Brady to non-Brady states.

Traffic Stop showed that the Brady Law had a disruptive impact on interstate gun trafficking from Brady to non-Brady states. Specifically, the study showed that states that began conducting background checks because of Brady were as much as 86% less likely to be sources of guns used in crimes in other states than they were prior to implementation of the law. Drs. Ludwig and Cook—who cite *Traffic Stop* in their paper—wrote:

> The best available evidence suggests that treatment state FFLs [Brady state gun dealers] are important sources of crime guns in both the treatment and control states. Interstate gun running is often the source of crime guns in the Brady control states, with many of these guns coming from states with more lax gun laws—such as the Brady treatment states.

Reducing crime and saving lives

Q: So, what is the evidence that Brady, by reducing the supply of crime guns, has reduced criminal gun use?

A: Another study released by the Center to Prevent Handgun Violence [CPHV], *Saving Lives by Taking Guns Out of Crime* (July 2000), documents the decline in gun use by violent criminals since 1994, coinciding with introduction of the Brady Law.

By analyzing crime data from the FBI's Uniform Crime Reports, the Center determined that the proportion of violent crimes committed with firearms rose steadily through 1993. In 1994, however, coinciding with the implementation of the Brady Law, the trend reversed and gun-related crime has been dropping faster than the violent crime rate ever since. The Center used this data to estimate the number of lives saved since Brady took effect—not because the crime rate was falling, but because the percentage of violent crimes committed with guns was falling.

The results of this analysis provide compelling evidence that the

Brady Law is saving lives by taking guns out of crime: from 1994 through 1998, an estimated 9,368 fewer people died than expected because the percentage of robberies and assaults committed with firearms fell each year after reaching a peak of 42.4% of robberies and 25.1% of aggravated assaults in 1993. Furthermore, from 1991 through 1993, an estimated 3,105 more people lost their lives in gun-related crime than expected because the proportion of assaults and robberies that involved guns increased each year from 1990 through 1993.

Q: How do you square the Ludwig/Cook paper with CPHV's assertion in Saving Lives *that Brady has in fact saved lives? Aren't the two papers' findings contradictory?*

A: No, the conclusions drawn from the Ludwig/Cook paper are consistent with the conclusions drawn from the Center's study. Remember, the Ludwig/Cook study says that the impact of the Brady Law is no bigger or smaller in the states that implemented the law than it was in non-Brady states. The Center's research shows that violent gun crime fell in association with the implementation of Brady—and because robberies and assaults committed with firearms are far more likely to result in a victim's death than similar crimes that do not involve guns, the decline in gun crime associated with Brady resulted in an overall drop in homicides beyond what was expected from the drop in the crime rate.

The Brady Law is saving lives by taking guns out of crime.

The Center's study shows the overall impact of the Brady Law. The implication of the Ludwig/Cook study is that Brady's impact was national, not localized to just Brady states. This conclusion is, in fact, supported by the Center's research. The Center showed that the impact of Brady on the use of guns in robberies and assaults was similar in both Brady and non-Brady states suggesting that the impact on homicide rates would also be similar.

Q: So what are the policy implications of the Ludwig/Cook paper?

A: Drs. Ludwig and Cook assert that the effectiveness of the Brady Law is undermined by the unregulated secondary market—a position that CPHV and Handgun Control have long held. Even though there is strong evidence that, because of the Brady Law, there are fewer guns available to criminals, there has been a reduction in the criminal use of guns, and these effects have prevented thousands of homicides from occurring, it is also true that gun crime would be further reduced if we regulated the currently unregulated secondary market. The simple fact that we do not require background checks on private gun sales and do not register guns contributes enormously to the existence of the illegal gun market—enabling criminals to acquire guns and to break the link between themselves and their use of firearms. If we closed this giant loophole in our gun laws by regulating the secondary market, the Brady Law would be even more effective and we would have less gun crime. However, that does not mean that the Brady Law is ineffective now.

12

The Brady Law Does Not Reduce Violent Crime

James Bovard

James Bovard is a columnist and an adjunct analyst at the Competitive Enterprise Institute, a Washington, D.C.–based public interest group dedicated to the principles of free enterprise and limited government. He is also the author of several books, including Shakedown: How Government Screws You from A-Z *and* Lost Rights: The Destruction of American Liberty.

The Brady Law—which requires a background check before a gun can be purchased—has not been an important factor in reducing crime. Supporters have exaggerated the number of people who have been prevented from buying guns, and the act has not prevented felons from purchasing guns illegally. According to statistics, states that are not covered by the law because they already had instant background checks have shown greater decreases in violent crime.

The Clinton administration is once again hailing the Brady Handgun Violence Prevention Act of 1993 as the key to national salvation. However, once again, the administration's claims are as bogus as a three-dollar bill. [The act was signed into law in 1993 and took effect the following spring.]

The Justice Department announced on June 21, [1998], that presale handgun background checks mandated by the Brady Law and by state laws resulted in 69,000 people being denied permission to purchase guns in 1997. But the Justice Department's estimates did not even maintain credibility for a week. The *Indianapolis Star* and *News* reported on June 24 that the Justice Department exaggerated by 1,300 percent the number of gun buyers turned down in Indiana because of the Brady Act. White House spokeswoman Nanda Chitre conceded the same day that President Clinton had exaggerated the number of people stopped from buying guns by the Brady Act and that White House counsel Rahm Emanuel had greatly exaggerated the number of newly bought guns used in homicides.

Unreliable data

This is not the first time that Clinton administration numbers on the Brady Act have gone down in disgrace. A 1996 General Accounting Office [GAO] report found that the data used to estimate nationwide denials under the Brady Act are extremely unreliable.

For instance, arrests are sometimes counted the same as convictions—and the fact that a person was once arrested (though later found innocent) could be used to deny his or her request to buy a firearm. GAO found that almost half of all the rejections under the Brady Act were due to paperwork problems or traffic violations, not to criminal records. (GAO did not even examine the percentage of denials that were valid).

Though the federal data is still very shaky, no member of Congress has requested that GAO update its study on Brady Act rejection numbers.

The Clinton administration is also deceptive in its claims that stopping felons from buying a gun in a gun store automatically stops them from acquiring a weapon. According to a 1991 Justice Department survey of convicts, most guns used to commit crimes have themselves been acquired illegally or on the black market.

Felons who attempt to purchase firearms can be sentenced to prison for 10 years. Yet despite Clinton administration claims on how dangerous illicit gun buyers are, the federal government prosecutes fewer than one in a thousand violators. The number of convictions from prosecutions for making false statements on Brady forms declined from 253 in 1994 to 36 in 1997.

Nor has the Justice Department kept records on the number of people who have successfully appealed denials to purchase handguns under the Brady Act. Paul Blackman of the National Rifle Association notes, "No one has a clue how many false positives are in the system. My guess would be that it would be somewhere in the neighborhood of three-quarters" of denials, based on the experience of state systems.

Nor has the Brady Act been a significant factor in reducing crime. Violent crime rates have declined more rapidly in states not covered by the Brady Act (because they have instant background checks, or for other reasons) than in other states. In fact, according to University of Chicago professor John Lott, author of the newly published *More Guns, Less Crime*, the Brady Act is actually responsible for "significant increase in rapes and aggravated assaults."

The dangers of a registration system

The Brady Act banned law enforcement agencies from using background check information to compile registration lists of gun owners. But some law enforcement agencies blatantly violate this provision of the law. National Rifle Association Vice President Neal Knox observed, "Some local and state agencies, such as the Ohio Bureau of Criminal Investigation and Identification, have been caught maintaining computerized records of Brady purchases despite the clear prohibition in the law. No prosecutions have resulted."

Even worse, the Federal Bureau of Investigation [FBI] recently announced its plans to retain records of approved gun buyers for 18 months.

The FBI's contempt for the clear language of the federal gun laws has enraged and alarmed many gun owners. In New York City, registration lists have been used by politicians to conduct witchhunts of peaceful gun owners. In many countries, registrations lists have been used to carry out gun confiscations.

> *Violent crime rates have declined more rapidly in states not covered by the Brady Act . . . than in other states.*

The Gun Owners of America, the nation's second-largest gun rights lobby, staunchly opposes any type of instant background check system because of fears that it will be contorted into a gun owners registration system.

Representative Bob Barr (Republican-Georgia) has introduced legislation to prohibit the FBI from compiling registration lists of gun owners and from imposing a fee to conduct federally mandated background checks on would-be gun owners. Representative Ron Paul (Republican-Texas) has gone further and introduced a bill (HR 2721) to completely repeal the Brady Act. Paul's bill would be a far better curative than Barr's bill, though with the current spineless majority in Congress, its prospects are not bright. [Neither bill was passed.]

The arguments over the effects of the Brady Act are drawing the battle lines for future political conflicts over gun control. The fact that the Clinton administration cannot get its numbers straight indicates that the ruling political elite have no right to restrict Americans' right to defend themselves and their families.

13

Targeting Illegal Firearms Trafficking Can Help Reduce Gun Violence

Bureau of Justice Assistance

The Bureau of Justice Assistance is a component of the U.S. Department of Justice's Office of Justice Programs. The bureau's goals are to reduce and prevent crime and improve the functioning of the criminal justice system.

Federal programs that target illegal firearms trafficking have been shown to reduce gun violence. These programs use three components. First, federal firearms licensees are notified about local regulations and are inspected for compliance. Second, several states have formed task forces that investigate the illegal sale, use, or acquisition of firearms. The final component includes a program that uses innovative projects, including a database program and a public information campaign, to reduce the level of illegal arms trafficking. A significant number of arrests and convictions have been made as a result of these programs.

This [viewpoint] provides an overview of the three components that make up the Firearms Trafficking Program and the promising practices and achievements of the eight demonstration sites. Detailed documentation of each site's work can be found in site summaries included in the appendixes. The following overview contains the background of each initiative, its goals and objectives, program elements, outcomes, lessons learned, and future directions. With the exception of Virginia, all funded projects were in operation as of late 1998 and were maintained with continuing Bureau of Justice Assistance [BJA] funds or through other sources.

Ensuring licensee compliance

In 1994, Congress changed the federal firearms licensing law to require ATF [Bureau of Alcohol, Tobacco, and Firearms] to ensure that licensees

From *Reducing Illegal Firearms Trafficking: Promising Practices and Lessons Learned,* by the Bureau of Justice Assistance, U.S. Department of Justice, Office of Justice Programs, July 2000.

are in compliance with state and local laws as a condition of receiving a federal firearms license.

The goal of this initiative is to enhance the ability of state and local law enforcement agencies to conduct more comprehensive background investigations on applicants for new or renewal federal firearms licenses. Programs in Oakland, California, and New York City were funded under this initiative, but other sites such as Santa Ana, California, funded under the Innovative Firearms Program, also established this goal. . . .

Oakland and New York developed programs that would reduce the number of federal firearms licensees, largely by bringing them into compliance with local, state, and federal regulations. In these cities, evidence indicated that some licensed dealers were violating the law by selling to prohibited persons, knowingly selling to straw purchasers, or selling guns "off book" out of their homes or the trunks of their cars. In both California and New York, increasingly violent gun crime was a significant issue that compelled these cities to focus on gun dealers.

Underlying the move to bring FFLs [federal firearms licensees] into compliance with local and state regulations were the fairly stringent regulations of all three cities. At the time BJA grants were awarded in Oakland and Santa Ana, city ordinances had already been passed to increase the number and severity of local FFL requirements. For example, in Oakland all FFLs have to apply for a local police permit, which involves a complete background check to rule out any prior criminal record, ethical breaches, or history of mental illness. The license fee in Oakland was increased to $500 every 2 years, and the licensee is required to maintain a minimum of $1 million in insurance. In Santa Ana, the license fee also increased, onsite inspections of dealer premises were mandated, and new security measures were required. In New York, while strict local requirements had been in place for some time, . . . BJA provided funds for the staff to conduct background checks for possible criminal history, mental health problems, and previous licenses or applications.

The lack of firearms legislation makes [West Virginia] a source state for firearms.

Program activities in these sites consist largely of informing new or existing FFLs about local requirements and mandates for compliance. These notifications frequently occur by mail, although police officers in New York sometimes pair with the Bureau of Alcohol, Tobacco and Firearms compliance inspector to make onsite visits. In all three cities, the notification system is effective because it is performed by local and federal representatives; it is particularly effective in New York where it is occasionally done in person. This combined effort by local and federal agencies ensures compliance and reduces the likelihood that applicants would mislead both agencies.

Once FFLs are aware of the city, state, and federal regulations and mandates, those not in compliance often willingly drop out of the licensing process. From 1994 to 1996, compliance work in Oakland reduced the number of firearms licensees from 57 to 6 (2 gun stores and 4 pawnshops). In New York, the program reduced the total number of FFLs from 987 in 1992 to 205 by 1996, a drop of 79 percent. In Santa Ana, compliance inspection resulted in a decrease from 90 FFLs to 13. Program staff in all three cities said they felt that the reduction in the number of licensees eliminated those who did not understand the purpose of the federal license (for example, some FFLs thought they needed a federal license to own a gun). It also eliminated some FFLs with unlawful intent.

An overview of the task forces

Several states (Indiana, North Carolina, Virginia, and West Virginia) formed task forces under this initiative to investigate individuals and dismantle organizations that were involved in the unlawful use, sale, or acquisition of firearms. Investigations of suspected traffickers have also been conducted in Oakland and Santa Ana (which were funded under other initiatives), and these sites followed a less formal task force approach. . . .

The goals of the four formal task forces developed through this program were targeting, investigating, and prosecuting individuals who engaged in firearms trafficking or who used firearms in violent crimes. The four sites followed a variety of approaches, ranging from small single-site task forces that predominantly pursued firearms traffickers to large multi-site programs that targeted violent career criminals.

Each program's approach consisted of a series of procedures to accomplish firearms trafficking investigations. These investigations generally included several steps, such as defining target populations, identifying these populations (using databases and local law enforcement contacts), selecting cases to pursue, determining which agency's staff should work on which case, collecting evidence, and preparing cases for prosecution. Each site developed slightly different procedures, which often reflected their different goals and objectives.

Indiana Task Force In Gary, Indiana, the single-site investigative task force targets multiple purchasers of firearms who are linked to criminal elements. All members of the task force are responsible for identifying targets for further investigation. To identify these crime gun sources, the investigators work with a database that they developed based on trace report information. Staff also search the database for names of individuals who buy firearms in large quantities that police later recover in connection with crimes. The task force also reviews the multiple sales forms, which FFLs send to ATF, to identify targets for investigation. However, receipt of this information is often delayed through dealer inadvertence or active resistance (for example, by sending ATF to the wrong location). The investigators also ask local police departments to alert them when they make arrests involving a seizure of multiple firearms, recover firearms with obliterated serial numbers, or handle cases involving a combination of firearms and drug charges.

In the five most violent areas of the city, the Gary task force also identifies and targets individuals who carry or use firearms during the course of violent crimes or while protecting their drug trade. These targets are developed through active investigation, historical data, Project Lead crime gun trace analysis, and confidential informants, as well as through intelligence provided by federal, state, or local authorities.

North Carolina Task Forces North Carolina maintains a statewide approach with six separate task forces targeting repeat violent offenders. These targets are identified through local law enforcement intelligence, whose cooperation is solicited through direct contacts and through policy department fliers . . . in police stations. Because of their extensive contact within the community, community policing officers and vice and narcotics squads are a tremendous resource for information about firearms-related crime and repeat offenders. Once identified, line-level investigators select targets for further investigation. The targets selected often include people with a history of violent crime, who are currently active in violent crime, and for whom there is a likelihood of successful prosecution under federal statutes.

A core group of task force personnel from the Federal Bureau of Investigation, the U.S. Secret Service, the Immigration and Naturalization Service (INS), the U.S. Drug Enforcement Administration (DEA), and local investigators participates in each target investigation. Investigators gather intelligence through extensive interviews of informants and surveillance of the subjects and their associates. Task force personnel also use sophisticated audio and video surveillance equipment; have access to special funds to purchase guns, drugs, and information; rely on informants; investigate personal and business assets; and conduct undercover operations. The key to these often lengthy investigations is patience and sufficient resources. Close working relationships with U.S. Attorneys, who provide ongoing input and assist in determining when a case is ready for trial, enhance case preparation. Task force staff also prepared a manual to document their best practices and have assisted other agencies in conducting similar investigations.

Virginia Task Forces In Virginia the effort was also statewide, with three separate task forces located in each ATF field division. The task forces were in operation from 1993 to 1996. In the first few years of operation, targets for investigations were predominantly identified by the Firearms Transaction Center (FTC), an agency tasked with conducting criminal background checks on all firearms purchasers. FTC notified the task force staff of any purchasers whose background was suspicious or incomplete and made their transaction records available to investigators to identify multiple purchasers and potential straw purchasers. Other investigations were initiated through local police contacts, including one large case that involved a dealer who sold 600 firearms without proper ATF documentation, many of which had obliterated serial numbers and were later recovered in New Jersey and New York.

The Virginia task forces pursued gun traces on all weapons recovered during their investigations and worked cooperatively with the National Tracing Center (NTC) and Project Lead to identify sources of crime guns. They also initiated investigations of FFLs in their jurisdictions who did not possess a state license. In general, the task forces were able to involve dealers as cooperative informants, some of whom even allowed surveillance in their stores. An additional unique source for investigations included members of a nearby hunt club who supplied information about suspicious firearms transactions.

West Virginia Task Force In another statewide effort, task force personnel in West Virginia conduct trafficking investigations, many of which involve guns-for-drugs operations. These operations are common in West Virginia primarily because the lack of firearms legislation makes the state a source state for firearms and, for a related reason, it is also a drug market state. A typical guns-for-drugs operation involves an individual who purchases weapons in West Virginia, transports them to firearms market states (such as New Jersey or New York), and sells them illegally at a large profit. The trafficker then purchases drugs in these states, which are source states for drugs, and returns to West Virginia to sell them, also at a huge profit.

Task force staff review firearms arrests and extensively debrief almost everyone who plea bargains out of federal court. These interviews are designed to identify firearms sources and targets for other investigations. In these cases, which are often related to narcotics charges, offenders often reveal gun-source information if asked in a casual way. The investigators also conduct interdiction efforts at bus, airport, and train terminals where they perform consent searches of people suspected of trafficking.

The firearms trafficking programs in the eight demonstration sites have significantly contributed to reducing firearms-related violence.

The task force solicits the assistance of other agencies and citizens to identify cases for further investigation. Members have worked with train station employees to alert them of travelers who go to and from source cities in a short timeframe, who buy tickets in cash, and who carry little or no luggage. The task force also trains state troopers on how to conduct field interviews to gain intelligence about firearms and encourages them to bring that evidence to the task force. In some cases, FFLs have also provided intelligence on straw purchasers; one even allowed a camera to be placed in his shop for surveillance.

California Task Forces Two additional sites, Oakland and Santa Ana, pursue trafficking investigations. In Oakland investigators target multiple firearms purchasers and straw purchasers. To identify targets, investigators use dealer reports of multiple sales, data from a ballistics imaging system, and crime gun tracing information. Law enforcement officials analyze this information to determine if certain individuals are operating as unlicensed dealers or to identify federally licensed dealers who may be making questionable sales. Most often, cases involve people who have purchased 12 or more guns in a 1-week period or who have purchased certain types of firearms that are typical to trafficking (low-cost weapons such as Lorcins and Brycos).

Early on, task force program staff trained Oakland Police Department beat officers and outside agencies on firearms trafficking issues and how to identify straw purchasers. These cooperating agencies now bring approximately 20 to 25 cases per month to each investigator on the task force team. In these cases, a task force investigator interviews the arrestee, initiates a trace of the weapon, performs followup investigative work, and, if appropriate, prepares a case for the district attorney. Two assistant U.S. Attorneys work directly with the task force on case preparation.

In Santa Ana, the Weapons Interdiction Team (WIT) also investigates suspected firearms traffickers, multiple handgun purchasers who may be associated with crime guns or trafficking, and straw purchasers. The team works with county and state agencies in areas where trafficking to or from Santa Ana is known to occur, develops relationships with informants, and analyzes data on firearms that are used in felony assaults. To support investigations and identify targets, the team transmits trace requests to NTC for all weapons the Santa Ana Police Department seizes on a daily basis and maintains a database of the findings from the trace reports.

The team also screens all pawn slips for weapons to determine which weapons have been stolen and to identify possible felons who may be pawning firearms. Team members develop case investigations using informants, undercover firearms purchases, and surveillance. Undercover contacts are developed through a review of arrest reports from the gang and weapons details and from the county jail booking sheets to identify individuals with gang affiliations or who are selling guns or drugs. One investigator works undercover in the jail and establishes a rapport with inmates for later undercover buys. The investigator attempts to learn as much as possible about where the inmates got the guns, whether they would be able to get more, and how he can be introduced to the sources.

The team identifies multiple gun purchasers (those buying more than five firearms within 5 days) through quarterly reports from California's Department of Justice and conducts background checks on them. These reports, called Multiple Handgun Purchase reports, are taken from the State of California Automated Firearms System, a database of all firearms sold statewide that is based on the dealer's record of sale (DROS).

Investigative task force results

For these varied and numerous task force operations, outcomes are often measured by the numbers of weapons seized and traced, cases initiated, arrests made, and convictions obtained.

As of April 1998, the Gary, Indiana, task force had seized 193 firearms, traced 2,694 firearms, initiated 132 investigations, and made 78 arrests (of which 36 resulted in conviction). The task forces in North Carolina have investigated 1,331 target cases since 1994. Of those, 64 are under review to determine whether they meet the qualifications for serious violent criminals, 214 are under investigation, 43 are pending arrest, 215 are awaiting prosecution, and 516 have been arrested and prosecuted; 279 cases were closed without arrest or prosecution.

From 1993 to 1996, the task forces in Virginia investigated 1,215 firearms violation cases, made 431 arrests, obtained 129 convictions (the remaining cases are pending in federal court), seized 397 firearms, and submitted 333 firearms traces to NTC. In West Virginia, from April 1994 through April 1998, the task force arrested 97 people on 152 firearms-related charges; 73 of the arrestees have been convicted and 55 of those have received punishments including some form of incarceration.

In Oakland, California, the investigative unit completed more than 3,000 firearms traces and developed relationships with informants whose leads have resulted in the investigation of at least 28 straw purchasers, 5 of whom were arrested and prosecuted. In Santa Ana, WIT made 41 arrests for trafficking (14 of which led to convictions), seized 55 weapons, and covertly purchased 61 weapons and 14 explosive devices.

Broader impacts of violent crime were measured in two sites: North Carolina and Santa Ana, California. Since the task forces began their work in 1992, the rate of violent crime in North Carolina has decreased by 13.8 percent and the murder rate has declined by 18.5 percent. This result is likely due to the combined efforts of several initiatives in the state. In Santa Ana, statistics show a reduction in firearms used in homicides from 93 percent in 1995 to 78 percent in 1997. In addition, gang-related homicides decreased from 48 in 1993 to 16 in 1997.

Innovative Firearms Program This initiative assists state or local jurisdictions in developing and implementing innovative projects designed to reduce the level of illegal firearms trafficking. Although both New Orleans, Louisiana, and Santa Ana, California, were funded under this initiative, only New Orleans' efforts are discussed in the section; Santa Ana's activities are discussed in previous sections. The project is unique because of its development of and reliance on technology to support law enforcement functions. The project combines the efforts of the New Orleans Police Department (NOPD), ATF, and a team of consultants from the University of New Orleans (UNO) to reduce the availability of crime guns—those used or possessed during the commission of a crime—and reduce the incidence of firearms-related crime in the New Orleans metropolitan area.

Several technologies support the program's activities in New Orleans. The first component is a database that codes the specific geographic location of trace report data on crime guns recovered in the city. The second component is the Integrated Ballistics Identification System (IBIS) that examines bullet and casing characteristics. . . .

The database program is designed to model the availability of crime guns in New Orleans and can be used to develop patterns of gun trafficking in the region. To develop this database, task force members asked local jurisdictions to submit trace requests on all firearms they recover at crime scenes or from victims. Trace reports returned with sufficient contact information about purchasers are investigated, which involves interviews and background checks to identify straw purchasers, people who are prohibited from purchasing firearms, and stolen firearms. Particular attention is paid to cases involving guns purchased in high-crime areas or purchases of two or more high-caliber weapons. The staff forward any information to NOPD for further investigation and enter data into the database for analysis of trends and patterns.

IBIS captures a computerized image of bullets and casings that have been test-fired from the firearms recovered by NOPD. These images are stored in a database for comparison of bullets and casings that have been collected in connection with other crimes. On several occasions, IBIS has linked a test-fired bullet or casing with an open investigation, leading to the identification of suspects.

New Orleans also instituted a successful public information campaign to identify sources of illegal guns. A telephone hotline was established to collect tips and other information on firearms and illegal sources, and a community education campaign was developed, which included inserting fliers into utility bills, producing television announcements, and meeting with the school board, neighborhood groups, and youth.

In New Orleans outcomes are measured by cases initiated and patterns identified. By October 1997, the task force had submitted trace requests for 2,850 weapons confiscated by NOPD. Trace report information from NTC was combined with intelligence gathering to support 370 firearms cases. These were turned over to local investigators for follow-up.

The database containing gun ownership histories of traced crime guns has been analyzed, and several patterns have emerged. For example, trace data developed over the first 2 years of the grant indicate that the majority of firearms confiscated by NOPD in the New Orleans metropolitan area were initially obtained through apparently legitimate means—from FFLs, pawnbrokers, or lawful transfers by unlicensed individuals.

Further investigation revealed that commercial and residential theft was the primary source of crime guns, which is in contrast to initial findings that straw purchases were the primary source. These crime guns are stolen from residences and businesses where firearms are maintained for a variety of reasons. Although in some instances these statistics may be slightly skewed because of errors in reporting, the data still support that stolen firearms are the primary source of crime guns.

The benefits of trafficking programs

The firearms trafficking programs in the eight demonstration sites have significantly contributed to reducing firearms-related violence. Their investigations of violent criminals, firearms traffickers, and straw purchasers have resulted in large numbers of arrests and convictions. The collaborations between local law enforcement agencies and ATF ensures that federal or state statutes are applied whenever appropriate, resulting in the toughest available sentences. The initiatives concentrate on ensuring FFL compliance with state and local requirements so noncompliant dealers can be identified and their businesses brought into compliance or closed. These efforts have resulted in significant reductions in the number of dealers likely to supply firearms to criminals.

These programs have also created unique information resources, improved other sources of information, and made available existing data that law enforcement previously had not used in trafficking investigations. These resources include information to identify dealers who supply weapons to criminals, multiple purchasers, or those associated with crime guns on a routine basis.

These programs have also fostered collaborative relationships among many agencies that do not typically cooperate with one another. This situation opens up avenues of significant information exchange.

The eight funded sites employed a wide range of investigative techniques to achieve their goal of eliminating illegal sources of firearms to reduce violent crime.

14

Enforcing Current Gun Laws Will Reduce Gun Violence

Benjamin Kepple

Benjamin Kepple is a journalist who serves as a senior writer for Heterodoxy *and as an education reporter for* Investor's Business Daily.

Unless they are strictly enforced, federal gun laws have little impact on crime. The National Rifle Association (NRA) has shown that the best way to reduce gun violence is to prosecute felons who attempt to purchase guns. For example, federal gun laws are strictly enforced in Richmond, Virginia, with the help of the NRA's Project EXILE program; as a result, murder rates have fallen sharply in that city. However, the Justice and Treasury departments have not acknowledged the success of Project EXILE and refuse to prosecute people whose violent felonies are revealed in background checks.

First the Million Mom March, whose philosopher-queen appeared to be Rosie O'Donnell. Then Charlton Heston, raising a rifle and challenging Al Gore to pry it out of his "cold dead hand."

Maybe America really is gun crazy, like people say. If so, there is one person who seems to make some sense. And it isn't Rosie or James Brady or the Vice President. It is, strangely enough, the gun controllers' worst nightmare, Wayne LaPierre.

"Let me tell you why I said it." LaPierre, executive vice president of the National Rifle Association, knew how to get the audience's attention in an appearance at the Wednesday Morning Club, a Los Angeles–based issues forum. It had been about a month since he strongly—and either famously or notoriously, depending on your point of view—attacked Bill Clinton on national television: "The President is willing to accept a certain level of violence . . . to further his agenda in this country." It was one of many punches that the National Rifle Association and the Clinton administration have traded back and forth in the increasingly apocalyptic debate over gun control. It wasn't the most diplomatic thing to say, yet LaPierre didn't retreat then and he wasn't retreating now. "The gun laws on the books are not enforced," he said. "The federal guns laws we have right now—there's a complete lack of enforcement. I've always thought we could save a lot of lives if we would enforce the laws against violent felons with guns, drug dealers with guns, and gangs with guns."

Of course, President Clinton had reacted to LaPierre's statement not by talking about federal gun laws but by telling the *Washington Post,* "Well, he could say that on television, I guess. But I'd like to see him look into the eyes of the mother of little Kayla Rolland." But that was disingenuous—no amount of gun control could have stopped a six-year-old boy from shooting dead Kayla, a fellow first-grader at a rural Michigan school, with a stolen weapon he found lying in a shoebox in the crackhouse where he lived with his uncle.

The exchange between LaPierre and Clinton made it clear the gun-control debate is not just a question of whether Americans should be able to own firearms to defend themselves, although that certainly is the major concern for the collection of individuals who have become known as "the gun lobby." It was played in the media as a *mano a mano* between the President and a representative of the gun world who dared attack him, but it actually raised the basic issue in the controversy of how to combat gun violence in this country. Do we pass laws to increasingly deny citizens access to guns, hoping that we can bring crime rates down, or do we allow Americans to have them in case they need to defend themselves, and focus on the "bad guys" rather than the law abiding citizens?

Unenforced gun laws

Neither side in this controversy can deny that the federal gun laws now on the books aren't doing much good at reducing crime and that one reason may be the administration's strategy to attempt to cut guns off at the source—"whatever that means," LaPierre quips—instead of prosecuting people who illegally carry or attempt to purchase weapons. He noted in his Wednesday Morning Club speech that out of the 6,000 cases of children taking guns to school [in 1999] that there were only thirteen prosecutions. Indeed, he points to a 1998 Syracuse University study, conducted by its Transactional Records Access Clearinghouse, that found that in 1997 and 1998 the federal government only prosecuted eleven people for transferring guns to minors, and only thirty-seven cases involving the illegal transfer of guns to felons.

LaPierre gave the National Rifle Association line, a line he articulates more smoothly and plausibly than anyone else in the anti-gun-control world, in a conversation with me from North Carolina, where the NRA was preparing for the convention that would lead to the Charlton Heston soundbite. "If they would just enforce the existing federal gun laws against violent criminals, drug dealers and gangs with guns . . . they would prevent these people from killing their next victim," he says. "[President Clinton] has the power to enforce the federal gun laws against violent criminals with guns. He won't do it."

The lack of enforcement of federal gun laws, LaPierre says, "is a deliberate and intentional strategy" of the administration. "The numbers show virtually no prosecution and no enforcement."

If it is an arguing point, it is a good one.

According to a study by scholars at Syracuse University, there are two cities in the United States where federal gun laws are strictly enforced— Richmond, Virginia, and Rochester, New York. That's due in large part to Project EXILE, a NRA-supported task force of federal, state, and local law enforcement bodies. (Texas has just announced that it will implement Project EXILE as well.) Noting that the murder rate in Richmond has fallen precipitously since Project EXILE's implementation, LaPierre asks, "Why should we just save lives in Richmond? Why not Los Angeles, or Washington D.C., or Chicago?"

In 1997 and 1998 the federal government only prosecuted . . . thirty-seven cases involving the illegal transfer of guns to felons.

But the Department of Justice isn't interested. Despite Project EXILE's successes, Deputy Attorney General Eric Holder has derided the program as a "cookie-cutter" approach to reducing crime, and said that it is "fundamentally wrong" to use federal monies to enforce federal gun laws in this way. La Pierre says that this reaction comes from the same Department of Justice which claims that it sees no relationship between incarcerating criminals and crime rates: "Tell that to any cop in America and they'll tell you that's hogwash."

In addition, the Treasury Department doesn't care for Project EXILE either, despite the fact that it's done quite well—in Richmond, the murder rate dropped 33% from 1997 to 1998. In fact, the numbers for 2000 look even better when compared with the past. *The Chicago Tribune* reports that in 1999, only 74 people were killed—the lowest rate in 15 years—and if this year's homicide rate stays constant, that number will be cut in half.

But Treasury's goal, to be achieved through the Bureau of Alcohol, Tobacco, and Firearms [ATF], is to "prosecute the few sharks at the top rather than the numerous guppies of the criminal enterprise." That's according to one ATF official attempting to explain away the fact that federal prosecutions of gun crimes have dropped 44% since President Clinton took office. But, as LaPierre remarks about the Kayla Rolland case, "a guppy is that case that happened in Michigan."

In that instance, the boy's uncle—who had carelessly left a loaded weapon in a shoebox—had a warrant out for his arrest and was under investigation by numerous law enforcement agencies—including federal agencies—but nothing was done. If the government had arrested him, it might have prevented that tragedy. And there was plenty of federal action after it happened—the man was charged with violating federal gun laws—but, as LaPierre notes, it was "a day late and a dollar short."

"The public needs to understand," LaPierre says, speaking of felons who attempt to purchase guns illegally, "that they are all walking the streets tonight." As LaPierre told the Wednesday Morning Club, there's no enforcement of the laws on the books when a felon goes into a store and illegally attempts to purchase a gun.

"Here's what happens under existing law when a violent felon walks into a gun store under the way Bill Clinton is administering (background checks)," he explained. "They do the check, they turn up the person as a violent felon trying to buy a gun. They say, 'OK, Clyde, we can't sell you the gun. But have a nice day—because we're not going to do anything to you except let you walk out that door.' Clyde is committing a brand-new federal felony when he tries to buy that gun—and yet the president says, 'I'm not going to prosecute anybody—the law was never meant to prosecute anybody.' So they let him walk out the door."

Prosecution equals prevention

So how to enforce the gun laws? The National Rifle Association, it will surprise some of its critics to discover, does favor gun laws, and although the ones LaPierre talks up aren't exactly draconian, it's difficult to disagree with him that a starting point in reconfiguring gun laws is to arrest felons that are either in possession of, or attempting to purchase, firearms and sentence them to jail time. When one considers that many of these criminals, after being turned away from gun shops, obtain their weapons elsewhere and go on to commit crimes, arresting them on the spot and reacquainting them with the criminal justice system doesn't sound like a bad idea. On a cost effective basis, who are the people most likely to be committing mayhem with the guns they have, a duck hunter or a strong arm robber with a previous record?

You might call it the "broken window" of gun violence. The original broken window theory, the brainchild of UCLA sociologist James Q. Wilson, suggests that in order to reassert the primacy of law and order into society, you begin by getting control over the actions of petty lawlessness—broken windows—which undermine the rule of law and begin the spiral into heavy crime. New York City Mayor Rudy Giuliani changed the social atmosphere of New York, for instance, by going after the squeegee men and turnstile jumpers in the subway. (Such policing not only stops such acts but also sweeps up many habitual criminals with outstanding warrants.) There's no reason that arresting felons attempting to purchase guns couldn't put a comparable dent in crime, especially when one thinks about what those recidivism-prone felons might do if they got their hands on a gun. "I hear the President constantly talk about prevention," LaPierre says. "Prosecution is prevention. You're preventing them from committing another crime."

The politics of the gun debate

Such thinking goes against the grain. So does the position of one of LaPierre's allies, Texas assemblywoman Suzanna Gratia Hupp, whom the NRA deployed with maximum effect as a talking head during the Million Mom March. Hupp was eating lunch with her parents at a cafeteria in Killeen, Texas, in 1991 when a demented gunman drove his truck into the restaurant and then shot more than 40 people. Hupp's parents were among the 23 dead, an outcome she believes she could have prevented if she'd had the handgun she normally carried but had left in the car.

Hupp made much of the fact that states (like Texas) with a concealed handgun law have lower incidence of gun violence. Her position about the deterrent value of being personally armed was played as something of a man-bites-dog story during the Million Mom March, yet Hupp had her innings.

Not that the Clinton administration would consider her arguments any more than it would debate LaPierre over the issue of preventing gun violence by prosecuting those who break the laws now on the books. For the Clinton administration and for Al Gore too, this is a political issue rather than an issue of crime. And LaPierre is right in suggesting that in a perverse way, the spate of juvenile tragedies involving firearms has been a political godsend for an administration which holds nothing sacred. The statistic behind these tragedies is never quoted: children's accidental deaths, resulting from firearms, is down from a high of 428 in 1976 to a low of 138 in 1996, according to the Center for Disease Control.

Who are the people most likely to be committing mayhem with the guns they have, a duck hunter or a strong arm robber with a previous record?

The NRA has always been a leader regarding gun-safety, LaPierre says. "If the issue is preventing accidents with guns, education's the answer," he notes. "We've always supported trigger locks, before I ever heard of this issue in the media. We're supporting the legislation in Congress to re-quire mandated-by-law safety devices or locks with every gun sale," he continues. "What we've been opposed to,"—mandatory trigger locks—"is not a solution." What would happen if certain extreme gun-control forces had their way regarding trigger locks, and someone broke into your home and stole a gun without a trigger lock? "They want to hold the home-owner responsible for a federal felony," says LaPierre. "A locked door ought to be enough."

And let's not forget the President's hand wringing over the children. "The president talks about thirteen children a day dying—you hear it day after day. The media just—without even looking into it—picked it up. It's such a distortion," LaPierre told the Wednesday Morning Club.

The thirteen-a-day figure, he pointed out, also includes "violent gang members—14, 15, 16, 17, 18, and 19 [years old]. Everything they're doing with a gun is already illegal. We want them to get picked up off the streets, under the existing laws, to make them safe and make other people safe, and Bill Clinton and Janet Reno fight us every day on this."

Revitalizing the NRA

The battle between the President and the NRA is made more difficult, LaPierre says, because of the media. This is not an idle claim on his part, either, despite the stereotype of conservatives who gripe about a menac-ing liberal media. The Media Research Center, which tracks partisan bias in the news media, has pointed out that the NRA is routinely bashed by news networks, from CBS to CNN; that the national news networks are not only biased in favor of gun control but usually just ignore stories and statistics that might put guns in a good light (for example, the MRC

found that in the past two years, people who successfully defended themselves using firearms were mentioned only 12 times out of the 653 gun
policy stories aired on network news programs); and that out of 28 stories
on national news programs examining the escalating battle between the
President and the NRA—many featuring LaPierre's comments regarding
the President—only one mentioned President Clinton's claim that other
countries have lower gun death rates because they don't have an NRA.

LaPierre, embolded by the fact that he is still standing after duking it
out with the President, has a grandiose plan in which the NRA will become its own media. The drive he envisions features everything from
half-hour long infomercials to *First Freedom* magazine (a hard-news style
publication), to daily, live news broadcasts over their Internet site. "The
media stranglehold can now be broken. We don't need them anymore,"
he says, adding, "we're going to cover the stories that . . . you don't see
on ABC, NBC, and CBS." This view has a sort of "tomorrow-the-world"
tone, but in fact it suggests that the NRA is indeed not as down and out
as it is sometimes portrayed. Having added 200,000 members in the last
six weeks alone—and now boasting 3.6 million members, the organization is not prepared to go gently into that good night of gun control.

Whatever else that may be said about it, the NRA position cannot be
faulted for lacking clarity and consistency. The current gun-control debate, LaPierre says, "is a lot more about banning firearms from honest
folks than it has to do with making America safe . . . the endgame of the
Gores and Clintons is to destroy the Second Amendment." But he's hope-
ful about the future, because he doesn't think Americans are buying Clinton's message. "I just don't think that Americans will buy it that liberty
induces evil or that freedom induces crime," he says.

Wayne LaPierre is an effective spokesman for a view which, if national opinion samples are to be taken seriously, is out of step with present social trends. But it is also true that the death of the NRA has been
exaggerated. One of the few things that both sides agree about is that how
the issue of gun control is resolved will determine how much the America of the past will survive in the America that emerges from this debate.

Organizations to Contact

The editors have compiled the following list of organizations concerned with the issues debated in this book. The descriptions are derived from materials provided by the organizations. All have publications or information available for interested readers. The list was compiled on the date of publication of the present volume; the information provided here may change. Be aware that many organizations take several weeks or longer to respond to inquiries, so allow as much time as possible.

American Civil Liberties Union (ACLU)
132 W. 43rd St., New York, NY 10036
(212) 944-9800 • fax: (212) 869-9065
e-mail: aclu@aclu.org • website: www.aclu.org

The ACLU champions the rights set forth in the Declaration of Independence and the U.S. Constitution. The ACLU interprets the Second Amendment as a guarantee for states to form militias, not as a guarantee of the individual right to own and bear firearms. Consequently, the organization believes that gun control is constitutional and, since guns are dangerous, it is necessary. The ACLU publishes the semiannual *Civil Liberties* in addition to policy statements and reports.

Cato Institute
1000 Massachusetts Ave. NW, Washington, DC 20001
(202) 842-0200 • fax: (202) 842-3490
e-mail: librarian@cato.org • website: www.cato.org

The Cato Institute is a libertarian public-policy research foundation. It evaluates government policies and offers reform proposals and commentary on its website. Its publications include the Cato Policy Analysis series of reports, which have covered topics such as "Fighting Back: Crime, Self-Defense, and the Right to Carry a Handgun" and "Trust the People: The Case Against Gun Control," and the magazine *Regulation*.

Center to Prevent Handgun Violence
1250 Eye St. NW, Suite 802, Washington, DC 20005
(202) 289-7319
websites: www.cphv.org, www.gunlawsuits.com

The center is the legal action, research, and education affiliate of Handgun Control, Inc. The center's Legal Action Project provides free legal representation for victims in lawsuits against reckless gun manufacturers, dealers, and owners. The center's Straight Talk About Risks (STAR) program is a violence prevention program for adolescents. Its websites provide fact sheets and updates on pending gun lawsuits.

Citizens Committee for the Right to Keep and Bear Arms
12500 NE Tenth Pl., Bellevue, WA 98005
(206) 454-4911 • fax: (206) 451-3959
e-mail: www@ccrkba.org • website: www.ccrkba.org

The committee believes that the U.S. Constitution's Second Amendment guarantees and protects the right of individual Americans to own guns. It works to educate the public concerning this right and to lobby legislators to prevent the passage of gun-control laws. It publishes several magazines, including *Gun Week, Women & Guns,* and *Gun News Digest.*

Coalition for Gun Control
PO Box 395 Station D, Toronto, ON M6P 1H9
or 1301 Sherbrooke St. E., Montreal, QC H2L IM3
Fax: (416) 604-0209 (Toronto) or (514) 528-2598 (Montreal)
e-mail: 71417.763@compuserve.com (Toronto)
or cgc.montreal@compuserve.com (Montreal) • website: www.guncontrol.ca

The coalition is a Canadian organization that was formed to reduce gun death, injury, and crime. The Coalition supports possession permits and tougher restrictions on handguns. Its website provides information on firearms death and injury, illegal gun trafficking, and Canada's gun control law. The coalition publishes press releases and backgrounders.

Coalition to Stop Gun Violence (CSGV)
1000 16th St. NW, Suite 603, Washington, DC 20002
(202) 530-0340 • fax: (202) 530-0331
e-mail: webmaster@csgv.org • website: www.csgv.org

The CSGV lobbies at the local, state, and federal levels to ban the sale of handguns to individuals and to institute licensing and registration of all firearms. It also litigates cases against firearms makers. Its publications include various informational sheets on gun violence and the *Annual Citizens' Conference to Stop Gun Violence Briefing Book.*

Handgun Control, Inc.
1225 Eye St. NW, Suite 1100, Washington, DC 20005
(202) 898-0792 • fax: (202) 371-9615
website: www.handguncontrol.org

A citizens' lobby working for the federal regulation of the manufacture, sale, and civilian possession of handguns and automatic weapons, the organization successfully promoted the passage of the Brady Bill. The lobby publishes the quarterly newsletter *Progress Report* and the book *Guns Don't Die—People Do* as well as legislative reports and pamphlets.

Independence Institute
14142 Denver West Pkwy., Suite 101, Golden, CO 80401
(303) 279-6536 • fax: (303) 279-4176
e-mail: webmngr@i2i.org • website: www.i2i.org

The institute is a pro–free market think tank that supports gun ownership as both a civil liberty and a constitutional right. Its publications include issue papers opposing gun control, such as "Children and Guns: Sensible Solutions," "'Shall Issue': The New Wave of Concealed Handgun Permit Laws," and "Unfair and Unconstitutional: The New Federal Gun Control and Juvenile Crime Proposals," as well as the book *Guns: Who Should Have Them?*

The Lawyer's Second Amendment Society
1077 W. Morton Ave., Suite C, Porterville, CA 93257-1989
e-mail: cyrano@ix.netcom.com • website: www.thelsas.org

The society is a nationwide network of attorneys and others who are interested in preserving the right to keep and bear arms. It attempts to educate citizens about what it believes is their inalienable right, provided by the Constitution's framers, to defend themselves with firearms if necessary. The society publishes the *Liberty Pole* newsletter six times a year.

National Rifle Association of America (NRA)
11250 Waples Mill Rd., Fairfax, VA 22030
(703) 267-1000 • fax: (703) 267-3989
website: www.nra.org

With nearly three million members, the NRA is America's largest organization of gun owners. It is also the primary lobbying group for those who oppose gun control laws. The NRA believes that such laws violate the U.S. Constitution and do nothing to reduce crime. In addition to its monthly magazines *America's 1st Freedom*, *American Rifleman*, *American Hunter*, *InSights*, and *Shooting Sports USA*, the NRA publishes numerous books, bibliographies, reports, and pamphlets on gun ownership, gun safety, and gun control.

Second Amendment Foundation
12500 NE Tenth Pl., Bellevue, WA 98005
(425) 454-7012 • fax: (425) 451-3959
e-mail: www@saf.org • website: www.saf.org

The foundation is dedicated to informing Americans about their Second Amendment right to keep and bear firearms. It believes that gun-control laws violate this right. The foundation publishes numerous books, including *The Amazing Vanishing Second Amendment*, and *CCW: Carrying Concealed Weapons*. The complete text of the book *How to Defend Your Gun Rights* is available on its website.

U.S. Department of Justice
Office of Justice Programs
PO Box 6000, Rockville, MD 20850
(800) 732-3277
e-mail: askbjs@ojp.usdoj.gov • website: www.ojp.usdoj.gov/bjs/welcome.html

The Department of Justice strives to protect citizens by maintaining effective law enforcement, crime prevention, crime detection, and prosecution and rehabilitation of offenders. Through its Office of Justice Programs, the department operates the National Institute of Justice, the Office of Juvenile Justice and Delinquency Prevention, and the Bureau of Justice Statistics. It publishes a variety of crime-related documents, including *Background Checks for Firearm Transfers, 1999* and *Firearm Injury and Death from Crime, 1993–97*.

Violence Policy Center
1140 19th St., NW, Suite 600, Washington, DC 20036
(202) 822-8200 • fax: (202) 822-8205
website: www.vpc.org

The center is an educational foundation that conducts research on firearms violence. It works to educate the public concerning the dangers of guns and supports gun-control measures. The center's publications include the reports *Handgun Licensing and Registration: What it Can and Cannot Do* and *Guns for Felons: How the NRA Works to Rearm Criminals*.

Bibliography

Books

Jack Anderson	*Inside the NRA: Armed and Dangerous.* Beverly Hills, CA: Dove Books, 1996.
John M. Bruce and Clyde Wilcox	*The Changing Politics of Gun Control.* Lanham, MD: Rowman & Littlefield, 1998.
Philip J. Cook and Jens Ludwig	*Gun Violence: The Real Costs.* New York: Oxford University Press, 2000.
Osha Gray Davidson	*Under Fire: The NRA and the Battle for Gun Control.* Iowa City: University of Iowa Press, 1998.
Tom Diaz	*Making a Killing: The Business of Guns in America.* New York: New Press, 1999.
Jan E. Dizard, Robert Merril Muth, and Stephen P. Andrews Jr., eds.	*Guns in America: A Reader.* New York: New York University Press, 1999.
Harry Henderson	*Gun Control.* New York: Facts On File, 2000.
Jacob G. Hornberger and Richard M. Ebeling, eds.	*The Tyranny of Gun Control.* Fairfax, VA: Future of Freedom Foundation, 1997.
Trudy A. Karlson and Stephen W. Hargarten	*Reducing Firearm Injury and Death: A Public Health Sourcebook on Guns.* New Brunswick, NJ: Rutgers University Press, 1997.
Don B. Kates Jr. and Gary Kleck	*The Great American Gun Debate: Essays on Firearms and Violence.* San Francisco: Pacific Research Institute for Public Policy, 1997.
Gary Kleck	*Targeting Guns: Firearms and Their Control.* New York: Aldine de Gruyter, 1997.
John R. Lott Jr.	*More Guns, Less Crime: Understanding Crime and Gun-Control Laws.* Chicago: University of Chicago Press, 1998.
Maryann Miller	*Working Together Against Gun Violence.* New York: Rosen, 1997.
Peter Squires	*Gun Culture or Gun Control: Firearms, Violence, and Society.* New York: Routledge, 2000.
Mary Zeiss Stange and Carol K. Oyster	*Gun Women: Firearms and Feminism in Contemporary America.* New York: New York University Press, 2000.
Josh Sugarmann	*Every Handgun Is Aimed at You: The Case for Banning Handguns.* New York: New Press, 2001.

William Weir	*A Well-Regulated Militia: The Battle over Gun Control.* North Haven, CT: Archon, 1997.

Periodicals

Charles L. Blek Jr.	"Our Second Amendment," *Human Rights*, Fall 1999. Available from 750 North Lake Shore Dr., Chicago, IL 60611.
Fox Butterfield	"Limits on Power and Zeal Hamper Firearms Agency," *New York Times*, July 22, 1999.
Congressional Digest	"Firearms in America: The Link Between Guns and Violence," November 1999.
E.J. Dionne Jr.	"Fear of Gun Control," *Washington Post National Weekly Edition*, June 28, 1999. Available from 1150 15th St. NW, Washington, DC 20071.
Robert Dreyfuss	"Dark Days for Gun Control," *Rolling Stone*, September 2, 1999.
Hillel Goldstein	"I'm Alive, No Thanks to Gun Control," *New American*, July 17, 2000. Available from 770 Westhill Blvd., Appleton, WI 54914.
Issues and Controversies On File	"Gun Control," July 14, 2000. Available from 11 Penn Plaza, New York, NY 10001-2006.
Issues and Controversies On File	"Gun Industry Lawsuits," October 15, 1999.
Michael Janofsky	"Attacking Crime by Making Federal Case of Gun Offenses," *New York Times*, February 10, 1999.
Bronwyn Jones	"Arming Myself with a Gun Is Not the Answer," *Newsweek*, May 22, 2000.
Kenneth Jost	"Gun Control Standoff," *CQ Researcher*, December 19, 1997. Available from 1414 22nd St. NW, Washington, DC 20037.
Wendy Kaminer	"Second Thoughts on the Second Amendment," *Atlantic Monthly*, March 1996.
David B. Kopel	"Taking It to the Streets: Treating Guns Like Cars," *Reason*, November 1999.
Daniel Lazare	"Your Constitution Is Killing You," *Harper's*, October 1999.
Eli Lehrer	"Cities Combat Violent Crime," *Insight on the News*, July 19, 1999. Available from 3600 New York Ave. NE, Washington, DC 20002.
John R. Lott Jr.	"Gun Control Advocates Purvey Deadly Myths," *Wall Street Journal*, November 11, 1998.
Jens Ludwig and Philip J. Cook	"Homicide and Suicide Rates Associated with Implementation of the Brady Handgun Violence Prevention Act," *Journal of the American Medical Association*, August 2, 2000. Available from 515 N. State St., Chicago, IL 60610.

Nelson Lund   "Taking the Second Amendment Seriously," *Weekly Standard*, July 24, 2000. Available from 1211 Avenue of the Americas, New York, NY 10036.

Brendan Miniter   "'Smart' Gun Technology Not So Smart After All," *America's 1st Freedom*, June 2000. Available from 11250 Waple Mills Rd., Fairfax, VA 22030-9400.

Grover G. Norquist   "Have Gun, Will Travel," *American Spectator*, November 1998.

Iver Peterson   "'Smart Guns' Set Off Debate: Just How 'Smart' Are They?" *New York Times*, October 22, 1998.

Steven Riczo   "Guns, America, and the Twenty-First Century," *USA Today*, March 2001.

Steven Schnur   "Guns Are Designed to Kill and They Do; By Allowing Their Manufacture and Use We Condone Death," *Christian Science Monitor*, June 17, 1999.

Kenneth Smith   "Gun Control That Works," *Reader's Digest*, November 1999.

Jeffrey R. Snyder   "Easing Handgun Licensing Laws: Helping the Public Fight Back," *USA Today*, September 1998.

Jacob Sullum and   "Cold Comfort," *Reason*, January 2000.
Michael W. Lynch

Michael W. Warfel   "Why Gun Control?" *America*, April 15, 2000.

Index

109

Nazis, 25
  gun seizure operations carried out by, 19–20
New Jersey, 61, 92, 93
New Orleans, 67, 95, 96
New Republic (magazine), 80
Newsweek (magazine), 33
New York City, 18, 27, 29, 88
  East Harlem, 22
  gun licensing restrictions in, 90–91
  mayor of, 100
New York State, 61, 83, 91, 93, 99
New York Times (newspaper), 30, 37
  poll, 65
North Carolina, 52, 91, 92, 98
  and gun trafficking task force, 94, 95
Norway, 32

O'Donnell, Rosie, 97
Ohio, 83, 87
Oregon, 29, 40, 41, 69

Pennsylvania, 41, 61
Pittsburgh, 8–9, 34
police, 37, 49, 53, 81, 92
  and Atlanta Police Department, 80
  and failure to protect citizens, 26
  gun control favored by, 12
  and operations against gun trafficking, 94–96
Police Foundation, 64
Port Arthur, Australia, 6, 7
Project EXILE, 99

rape, 41, 43, 44, 80
  decrease in, associated with concealed-carry laws, 15
  increase in, associated with Brady law, 87
Reagan, Ronald, 6, 29
Rehnquist, William, 20
Richmond, Virginia, 12, 99
right-to-carry laws. *See* laws, concealed-carry
robbery, 20, 27, 41, 42, 80
  drop in rates of, 32
  due to concealed-carry laws, 15
  increased rates of, in Australia, 7
  use of guns in, 10, 49
  reduced by Brady law, 85
Robinson, Krista D., 58
Rochester, New York, 99
Rolland, Kayla, 98, 99
Rosen, Gary, 27
Russia, 17
Rwanda, 25

Saturday Night Special, 26, 29, 37
  as defensive weapon of the poor, 18, 34
Schlafly, Phyllis, 14
Secret Service, U.S., 92
shootings
  of Japanese student, 39
  at Jewish community center, 9
  in schools, 7, 18–19, 69
  see also mass shootings; *specific locations of shootings*

Sharn, Lori, 45
Siebel, Brian J., 67
60 Minutes (TV news program), 71
Smith & Wesson, 69, 71–72, 74
Springfield, Oregon, 69
Stewart, Ron, 70
Sudan, 25
suicide, 30, 33, 59, 68, 73
  and availability of guns, 32
  guns used in approximately half the cases of, 10
  leading cause of firearm-related death in America, 64
  by teens, 65
Supreme Court, U.S., 12, 21, 62
Switzerland, 17, 32
Syracuse University, 98, 99

Targeting Guns (Kleck), 35
Teret, Stephen P., 58
tobacco industry, 67–68
To Keep and Bear Arms (Malcolm), 23
Traffic Stop (Center to Prevent Handgun Violence), 84
Traficant, James, 17–18
trigger locks, 15, 37, 60, 66, 81

United States, 39, 43
  defensive gun use in, 49
  gun control unrealistic in, 15, 18
  gun ownership in, 11, 13, 24
    changes in, 28–29
    linked to freedom, 19
    mostly revolvers, 64
  gun violence in, 10
    high rate of death from, 6, 9
  homicide rates in, 24
  and Jim Crow south, 25, 34
  low rate of "hot burglaries" in, 39
  reasons for high crime rates in, 25
  and urbanization, 10
U.S. v. Verdugo-Urquidez, 20

violence, domestic, 17
Violence Policy Center, 30, 63, 66, 75
Virginia, 89, 91, 92, 94, 99

waiting periods, 17, 29, 43
Washington, D.C., 16, 29, 36
Washington Post (newspaper), 7, 98
Weapons Interdiction Team (WIT), 94–95
Webster, Daniel, 48
Wednesday Morning Club, 97–99, 101
Weekly Standard (newspaper), 34
West Virginia, 91, 92–93
Wilson, James Q., 100
women, 43
  guns helpful for, 17, 20

Youth Crime Gun Interdiction Initiative Trace Analysis Reports (Bureau of Alcohol, Tobacco, and Firearms), 84
Yugoslavia, 25